# Missing More Than Music

## When Disputable Matters Eclipse Worship and Unity

Danny Corbitt

For Davie Naugle

authorHOUSE®

*AuthorHouse*™
*1663 Liberty Drive, Suite 200*
*Bloomington, IN 47403*
*www.authorhouse.com*
*Phone: 1-800-839-8640*

*First published by AuthorHouse     10/31/2008*

*ISBN: 978-1-4343-4359-8 (sc)*

*Printed in the United States of America*
*Bloomington, Indiana*

*This book is printed on acid-free paper.*

# Table of Contents

♪

## Exclusion's First Disputable Matter: "God Commanded the Early Church to Chant."

♪

## Exclusion's Second Disputable Matter: "Texts on 'Worship' Only Apply to Christian Assemblies"

♪

## Exclusion's Third Disputable Matter: "The New Testament is Silent on Singing Praise with Any Accompaniment"

Exclusion's Fourth Disputable Matter: "The New Testament is Silent on Singing or Listening to Solos"

Exclusion's Fifth Disputable Matter: "God Desires Division When we Disagree over Praise"

# Foreword

It's about time someone wrote a book like this. Few scholarly books have been written about instrumental music in worship. And very few have been written with an open mind regarding the outcome of the research. Danny Corbitt has had convictions on both sides of this issue. And as a result of his desire for truth, he studied this topic more fully than anyone I know. Because of his personal journey and background, we get not only an in-depth treatise of a controversial subject but also the development of thought of an honest seeker.

I've never met a kinder person than Danny Corbitt. That's why this book rings true to me. Danny doesn't have an axe to grind, and he is not mad at anyone. He simply loves God and wants to worship Him more and in whatever way he can. Ultimately, leading people to a better understanding of the freedom we can experience in worship is the purpose of this book.

When I studied this subject in the past, Danny was the first person I would contact for information. No one knows more on this subject than Danny. Every time I talk to him I learn more. He is always telling me new facts that I have never heard of before.

For some of you this book will be an eye opener. It will make you wrestle with long held beliefs. Others of you may not even understand why a book on this subject needs to be written. If that is the case, I still encourage you to read it because it will not only give you some interesting if not unusual history but also a way to approach any biblical subject in order to lead to gracious and thoughtful conclusions.

Thank you, Danny, for your commitment to tackle a subject that everyone tends to avoid. Thank you for being bold enough to tell the truth while at the same time revealing your heart. No work like this has been done previously. I think it will be the defining treatment of the subject, and in my opinion, we will not need another study on this matter.

In the long run, Danny's love for the Lord as demonstrated here will release many people from the constraints of their past and free them to worship God in spirit and truth. For this freedom, I am indeed grateful.

Milton Jones
December, 2007

# Acknowledgments

"I'd like to ask you not to tell anyone I'm reading your manuscript," he wrote, as he let me know that he had obtained a copy second-hand. I answered with the truth. I understood. His secret was safe with me. So is yours, in case you also are among those who will be reading this book behind closed doors.

Maybe my cover design should have been a brown paper bag.

Here I find myself writing thanks, but only for those whom I may acknowledge publicly. There have been others. Privately, I have thanked scholars and others who reviewed my work, confirmed it, and offered encouragement, though they will not be mentioned here. I could not have had the confidence to go forward without them.

In the public arena, I especially thank God for several who read my earliest manuscript several years ago, when it was so very hard to read, when only a selfless friend would have trudged through it. Terry Cagle is one of those. He confirmed that I was headed in the right direction and making good sense. He encouraged me to add the chapter about my journey, to share myself with my readers. In time, he also found others who would read the work and add their encouragement and feedback.

Milton Jones saw my rough early attempt and never gave up on me. He warned me that if my book ever went to print, then I would need every friend I could find. He has always been that true friend. He has planted seeds and let me run with them. His voice both to me and on my behalf has been invaluable time and again.

I thank God most of all for my wife of over 20 years. Cindy loves audio books; she hates to read. But she sat with me and read my earliest work; she volunteered. Again and again, she would ask, "What are you trying to say here?" When I answered, she would blink and say, "Then why didn't you just say that?" She freed my manuscript from lofty language to plain talk that people could understand without getting a headache. I can't thank God enough for her, and certainly not just for her help with a book.

Jim Beebe is an elder and student of the word who believed in me and was among those who first encouraged me to get my work published. When things seemed to be collapsing, Victor Knowles and Charles Dailey supported me with just the right words. Davie Naugle abandoned himself to the brave conviction that God is able. I am also thankful that God led my family to Christ Community Church, where we could heal and grow.

I am thankful for the trials God used to guide my work. I am thankful that worship and unity came into painfully sharp focus in the college ministry I served, so that I could no longer avoid the topic. I am thankful that my church experience forced me to examine God's heart for our assemblies as I never would have otherwise. I am thankful that Church of Christ publishers agreed with my conclusions but could not publish my work,[1] because the repeated process focused my thoughts.

The last one I thank God for is you. Thank you for giving this book a hearing, especially if you must read it wrapped it in a brown paper wrapper. When you're done, I hope that you will be one of those friends who will remain when friends are hard to find. If it blesses you, then I pray that you will share what you have learned with someone you love who has been missing more than music.

---

[1] One publisher would not read my manuscript because "church politics would never allow me to print it." A former publisher explained that it would be "commercial suicide" for anyone in the restoration movement to publish my work.

# My Journey

"Will our children praise with instruments?" She prayed the answer was no, but the question exposed her greatest fear for the church of tomorrow. She asked me because I was in a position to see some evidence, maybe even to be held accountable. I had worked as a campus minister at one of the largest universities in Texas for the preceding 14 years. We had mobilized scores of Christians from the surrounding cities and were baptizing students from all corners of the world who had come to our college to study. As I concluded my report to her church that night on God's amazing outreach to the lost on our campus, her one burning question remained. "Is the church of tomorrow listening to the church of yesterday on musical instruments?"

If your background is in the Churches of Christ, then you probably didn't notice that her question was off topic. Among us, it is not uncommon for questions about how we sing praise to surface in discussions on completely different subjects. For us, *how* we praise is a consuming subject. One's opinion on the use of instruments or solos in praise is a litmus test for church staff candidates or missionary support. It can be a sticking point for prospective Sunday school teachers. Many consider one's view on this issue to be a significant test for Christian fellowship.

At the same time, our young adults especially are more and more inclined to listen to Christian, instrumental music groups. Some preachers among us are leading a call for acceptance and fellowship with "instrumental" churches, though the progress toward unity is hampered by a fear of increasing the tension over praise. In these days, we've seen many abandon the Churches of Christ; many are fearful. The energy we expend on our distinct, external practice in praise is consuming. It prevents us from progressing deeper into the heart of praise. It robs us of energy to explore other issues, as well.

Is there more to worship than merely being right about instruments? It seems hard for us to say. A discussion of worship among us often stalls on our preoccupation with "congregational, *a cappella*" singing. Our overriding attention to the debate over instruments and solos leads us to examine praise passages with an eye focused on that single question. It is as though praise scriptures had no deeper purpose than to weigh in one way or the other on *our* issue.

This book, then, is more than an evaluation of the use of instruments, clapping, solos, and choruses in praise to God. It seeks a deeper understanding of God's heart for our praise. It desires to reinforce the place of praise in our *daily* lives and to renew special blessings in our assembled praise. It stresses that our praise is missing things more important than guitars and choruses.

It asserts that our unity is suffering as well. You see, the way we handle our disagreements over music is so central to us that it has become our pattern for handling disagreement in every aspect of Christianity. Re-examining the *way* we differ over praise reopens the door to unity. Indeed, our fellowship cannot re-evaluate unity without another look at our differences over praise. The two greatest issues confronting the *a cappella* Churches of Christ are inseparably entwined, and must be untangled together.

Strangely, the two issues we most desire to examine – worship and unity – are the most difficult for us to freely examine. They are our most sensitive issues. In practice, we have a tendency to question not just the credentials, but even the moral character of anyone who would write on the wrong side of our topics (where "wrong" means the opposite view to one's own). Perhaps, then, you first need to know a little about me and why I believe God has spent a lifetime preparing me to write this book for you. Before you examine the message, maybe you should know a little about the messenger. This chapter is my story, my journey.

I grew up in what we call the restoration movement. In my childhood and adolescence, God allowed me to experience both its instrumental and its *a cappella* sides, first one, then the other. My earliest experience was at the local Christian Church. I have a five-year pin for one stretch when I never missed Sunday school unless I was sick in bed. Sometimes my mother would take my brother and me to the assembly, too. I loved Jesus. I was baptized there. I still remember the preacher sitting in our living room talking to my brother and me the night before we were baptized.

In the seventh grade, I began to attend the local Church of Christ. I remember the first assembly I attended and the strange feeling that came over me as I heard a large crowd singing *a cappella* for the first time in my life. I was just a kid, but I had a fearful feeling, as though I were at the mercy of a sort of a mob. I got used to the new way of singing. I became a member of that church a few years later. On that occasion, the preacher gave a sermon in prayer form, asking God's forgiveness for me, since I had come from a church that had used instruments.

I was in the school band, and I played the guitar. The church youth minister saw my musical talent, and groomed me into quite a song leader. I led songs at our youth gatherings and on our bus and in our weeklong summer campaigns. While I learned to sing harmony, my best friend made me sit on his deaf ear side. My senior year of high school, I became a drum major in the band, and I graduated to leading singing sometimes on Sundays. At first, I found that keeping the marching band together was easier.

My freshman year of college, a classmate invited me back to a Christian Church for a Gospel Meeting. As I heard accompanied congregational singing again for the first time in six years, I felt very uncomfortable, and a sense of *déjà vu* swept over me. I realized that my comfort with instrumental accompaniment in church was based, at least in part, on what I was used to.

In college at a state school, I helped to host an evangelistic, weekly Bible study in my dormitory for three years. I saw many of my friends reborn. In my four undergraduate years, our campus ministry saw 75 baptized into Christ, and we weren't a part of the Crossroads / Boston Movement.

For some of my friends, becoming a Christian was especially costly. One of my friends knew that her decision for Jesus meant that her family would disown her. (A few years later, her father even refused to walk her down the aisle in her wedding.) The night of her baptism, before we headed to the church, I sat in my dorm room asking myself what I had done. I remembered that Jesus said that he would have that effect on families. God reminded me that I could only call people to what I was certain that he had said. So, I never taught *a cappella*; I avoided the topic as much as possible.

After graduation, I spent two years as a missionary apprentice in Santiago, Chile, in South America. I trained at Abilene Christian University and went out as a part of their MARK program. (My lead missionary joked that the program was named after the first missionary apprentice failure, John Mark.) I studied under some godly professors, men held in well-deserved respect.

As a missionary apprentice in Chile, I found myself studying things I had always taken for granted, like why we use *unleavened* bread in the Lord's Supper. I was led to look at instruments again. We sang *a cappella*, but I couldn't teach on it.

Soon after my return, I became the "Church of Christ" campus minister at my state college alma mater. I held that position for 14 years. About the time I began, another ministry on our campus was having a huge impact. Their progress was arrested when their campus minister, Davie Naugle, let it be known that he did not hold to the premillennial view of his denomination. He was fired. When I went to see him, he surprised me by asking about my views on instrumental music. I told him that I didn't understand our arguments. I hedged by saying that maybe I just needed to study them more closely. Making no argument, he merely told me that he thought that I could make a great impact for the sake of my fellowship on that topic. He had earned the right to say that. I tucked it away.

Our university was one of the largest in Texas. Our international population numbered in the thousands. We began reaching them by using the Let's Start Talking (LST) material, which was actually designed for use in evangelistic campaigns overseas. The Chinese population on our campus was especially receptive. One of the first Chinese students to come to Christ told me that there was a hunger among his people. They didn't know if the answer they sought was Jesus or democracy or science, but they were certain that the answer was not communism. Our campus had students who had been in Tiananmen Square when the tanks rolled in. They knew that what they had was broken.

The LST people told us that ours was the first campus ministry to use their material on a U.S. campus. Their "FriendsSpeak" program was then born to pursue stateside opportunities like ours. As Jesus foresaw, the Chinese students were very interested in seeing Christian unity. The odds of them finding an anti-instrument fellowship when they returned to China were slim. I struggled with what we could teach them.

Of equal concern to me were the American students who were coming to college from our churches. Studies have shown that 4 out of 5 never get involved with a Church of Christ; half may never even visit one. Some arrive on our campuses looking for anything but a Church of Christ; they say they are looking for something "more spiritual."[1] Others are looking for anything but church, period. College doesn't cost them their faith; they arrive without any. They are indoctrinated, but not convicted.

Whether or not you agree with our opposition to instruments and choruses, you should know that most of our students who go away to college are not convinced. The rare exceptions, however, are sobering. One day a girl lamented to me that the late, popular Christian songwriter Rich Mullins was burning in Hell. Indeed, she feared that the authors of almost every song of praise that we sing today are Hell-bound because of their praise with instruments.

Students don't reach conclusions like this on their own; our churches train them. I had to take into account the role of views like our opposition to choruses and instruments in the exodus of the students from our churches. Right now, you may think that *whatever* I believe about instruments and choruses is wrong, but we must ask why our sons and daughters are most likely to leave our churches.

I'll mention one other student who brought me a booklet opposed to instruments, choruses, and solos, written by his new preacher. I took the first argument and showed the student how it was flawed. To my surprise, he shared my study with his preacher. To my greater surprise, the preacher said it looked like he couldn't use that argument any more. I wondered if there was hope.

God was convicting our students about praise regardless of the instruments. One example was our spring break mission trips. In Mexico, we found ourselves heart to heart with brothers and sisters who couldn't carry a tune, but praised with all their soul. We had to ask why our singing sounded more professional, but less passionate. Students also saw the resistance of some older Christians to singing newer Christian songs set to modern rhythms. We asked what God was looking for in a song of praise.

In my final years, our campus ministry began to work in cooperation with other Christian ministries on our campus. Our elders gave us that freedom. (God worked that out in an amazing sequence of events.) We began to discuss lots of important issues among ourselves. In our campus outreaches, we agreed not to call people to "ask Jesus into their hearts," but to put them in contact with Christians who could open God's word with them. Our involvement provided the opportunity to discuss issues like that. Once in a while we sang together, and sometimes there was accompaniment. As those concerned for the lost on our campus, we sharpened one another. We spoke openly out of our genuine, nurtured relationships. The unity of Christ was put at a premium.

I hope it is obvious that I love music. I'll add that I love harmony, and I love *a cappella* singing. Besides often leading the singing group of my campus ministry, I have led singing numerous times for Vacation Bible Schools. I have directed a chorus for my congregation at Leadership Training for Christ (LTC) many years. I'm not sure I have ever led a VBS or LTC group without teaching songs that I have written or arranged. I have taken scripture and put it to the music of the Backstreet Boys, Smashmouth, Avril Lavigne, or whomever the kids were listening to. I put the thoughts of Psalm 127 to my own music in a song for adults. Titled, "Wasting Time," it reminds us of what a waste of time it is to worry, when God is in control. I wrote it because I need to be reminded.

Because I write songs, I was especially pleased when one year, one of my LTC students asked me to teach her how to write a song. That year, our chorus sang the song that she had written, and her friends loved it. Sadly, I don't need all of the fingers of one hand to count the Christians I personally know in Churches of Christ who have written a song of praise. I believe that this book will explain why that is common.

I do not propose that instruments are any panacea for our singing; putting together a better concert experience for Christians is not my suggestion. In truth, I have seen assemblies where many people *never* sang, regardless of instruments. I do confess that I'd like to hear a purposeful solo every now and then. I just believe our assemblies are missing something more.

Campus ministers must maintain contact with all levels of church staff throughout the "feeder churches" to their campuses. In my 14 years as a campus minister, I was surprised to learn how many other ministers were privately unconvinced by our arguments. They knew that they could hold different views on just about any other topic, but it seemed that the emotions ran too high on instruments and solos to risk becoming a lightening rod if they spoke up.

A few years ago, I left supported ministry. I believe that God continued to prod me, to lead me along as I struggled with the issues. He let me suffer so that I could examine aspects of praise that I never dreamed of addressing. Davie Naugle's words never left me. The accountability to share what God was teaching me has remained inescapable. So, here is the fruit of my study. May it contribute to our understanding of these issues that divide us. In the end, may it lead us to richer worship and more perfect unity!

---

[1] Particularly the chapter titled, "When Listening to Praise is a Sin," will address some of these "spiritual" issues.

# What Happened to Praise
# When Jesus Came?

I t used to be different.

When the Red Sea swallowed Pharaoh and his chariots, Miriam led the Hebrew women with tambourines and dancing and a chorus of praise to God (Exodus 15:20, 21). David sang and made music with all his soul on the harp and lyre (Psalm 108:1, 2), and he wouldn't let his wife Michal shame him for his unbridled praise (2 Samuel 6:16, 21, 22). At times the people shouted or clapped their hands, musical instruments rang out, believers danced or fell to their knees, and hands were lifted high as God's people made a joyful noise.

And then Jesus came.

If you grew up in the Churches of Christ in the South (as I did) or in one of our mission points, then you were taught that the new covenant brought by Jesus changed praise. It probably made you uncomfortable (or maybe defensive) even to *read* the opening of this chapter with all of its varied references to praise as it once was … and as it once was commanded. We were taught that God doesn't want those kinds of praise any more. "Praising God the way *we* want doesn't matter; we must praise God as *he* desires," we were told. And we were taught what God desires … or, better said, what he rejects.

God's New Testament desire (specifically in regard to songs of praise) was condensed for us into two new laws:

1) God *no longer* approves of musical instrument accompaniment in songs of worship to him. Spoken words alone are now what he seeks.

2) God *no longer* approves of his people silently listening to any song sung by one or more other believers as acceptable worship.

## Not Knowing Why

We never read *why* God changed his mind about praise; it seems that no one knows for sure. Maybe it's not our place to ask. We struggle to put aside our concerns that neither Jesus nor his apostles *ever* so much as *mention* the change, much less explain it. We know why Jesus drove out the *moneychangers*, but we don't know why he would expel the *musicians*.

Before Jesus came, we wonder if God was merely tolerating the old ways of praise. We ask if God's people in those days were incapable or maybe even unworthy of praising Him the way he truly desired. Why did He embrace, even command, what is now exposed as "childishness." Why did God nail tambourines and harps, dancing, expressive hands, shouting, and sharing your song with the assembly to the cross? Or put another way, why did he ever request them at all?

Not knowing why makes it hard to know how to apply these new commandments. What is it about solos and instruments that God doesn't like? If he doesn't like solos, then how may I *teach* a new song in a way that pleases him? If God doesn't like non-verbal music, then what about clapping or hand motions in children's songs? Not knowing *why* forces us to wrestle – even among ourselves – with reasonable applications for these "implied" New Testament changes to praise.

Our deductions from scripture do not seem as obvious to others as they appear in our own eyes. Working with our children in college, I found that they have difficulty reconciling our music doctrine with our practice. If you have never asked our young adults what they believe we teach about instruments and solos, then you might be surprised to hear what they would say. If they believed they could answer you freely, here are some of the things they would say that we believe.

Regarding instruments:

- You can teach Christian songs with (unauthorized) clapping and hand motions to little children as long no one calls it worship. Singing these "Vacation Bible School" songs must never be mistaken for acceptable worship from either you or the children you have taught. Therefore, it must **never be done** in a Sunday morning church assembly.

- God allows you to attend weddings and funerals where musical instruments are used as long as you don't worship. (You may sing or listen to "How Great Thou Art" in these contexts as long as you don't mean it, they wonder?)

- You may use a musical instrument at home to help you learn or write a new song. It's okay provided you don't "worship" while you work with the instrument. A good rule may be not to think about the words until you finish learning the tune.

- It is not wise to listen to contemporary Christian music (i.e.: with instruments) on the radio. You might begin to consider it to be worship. God does not accept the worship of those singers. Given the choice, wise Christians prefer to let secular music or talk radio influence their thinking through the day.

- Harmonizing with words that "do not communicate" (like "ooh" or "ah") is not worship. When singing, you can only sing ooh or ah for a very brief time. (Verses on timing are elusive, but clearly to be obeyed.) Although *ooh* and *ah* are spoken words, they do not communicate meaning. (We must not consider Romans 8:26 or a dictionary as we reflect on that.) If *ooh* and *ah* are held out, then at some point they become like humming, which is like instruments or clapping, which cannot be used at all.

Regarding solos and choirs:

- You may write a song of praise and sing it as worship...if you are alone. If you sing it before others, however, it will no longer be acceptable worship. At best this "performance" is only "song teaching." It can become acceptable worship again when everyone present sings with you.

- Songs where the words are alternately sung and then echoed by different groups throughout are OK, even though everyone is not singing the same words at the same time. The echo can even have completely different words, as long as everyone sings throughout, but …

- It is wrong to have one group sing an entire song and then let everyone else echo that entire song. Although the scriptures *never* discuss (authorize?) echoes or their delay times, "short" delays are *surely* OK, but "long" delays define choruses, and are bad.

- Songs where some people (e.g.: the women or the altos) sing a verse or a line of the song by themselves – "Who like me Thy praise should sing?" or "Altos only on verse one" – *with no echo at all* (like a chorus) are okay (deemed not a chorus) as long as it is a short section of a long song. Singing that same verse as a chorus without the rest of the song would not be okay.

- You can participate in Christian weddings and funerals where soloists or choirs are heard. God accepts your silent affirmation of the prayers, but not the songs, unless you sing along with the soloist, etc.

If you feel insulted by this perspective of our practice, then I beg you to ask your adult children if it is accurate. I believe you will find that your argument is not with me. More than that, you must know that our opposition to instruments, solos, and choruses is inconsistent and self-contradictory for a reason. The argument of this book is not that we should do a better job of applying our rules. Rather, the argument of this book is that the rules cannot be applied in any other or better way, because our opposition is not founded in scripture as we have thought. Something has kept us from seeing.

## A *Cappella*-Colored Glasses?

Our friends outside of the Churches of Christ generally don't see what we see regarding solos, choruses, and instruments. We respond that either (a) they don't understand what the Bible says or (b) they care more for pleasing themselves than for pleasing God. We wonder how they don't understand, how they look at the same passages, the same Greek dictionaries (lexicons), and the same church history and don't find the same rules … at all. On the other hand, we see them die for Jesus, and we wonder if they really have a problem with submission.

It's not just that we understand praise differently from most of those *outside* of our fellowship. No, we also look at those same pages and have sharp disputes among *ourselves* about the interpretation of our rules. Not only do we claim that those *outside* of our movement cannot see, but we also claim that many (most?) of those *inside* our movement cannot see as well. Quietly we wonder if there's a problem with *our* reasoning or *our* submission.

Something is keeping a lot of sincere believers from reaching the same conclusions regarding praise. Since we disagree with Christ's church at large and even among ourselves, it is reasonable to ask if something is clouding *our* vision. Perhaps we are wearing a kind of glasses that color our view of praise, that keep us from seeing what the rest of Christianity sees. Perhaps our glasses come in varying shades, so that we cannot find consistent interpretation even among ourselves. Maybe we are the ones who cannot see. Perhaps we are wearing *a cappella*-colored glasses.

The conclusion of my study is that we are indeed wearing *a cappella*-colored glasses. We have accepted arguments that don't make good sense, but our glasses have kept us from seeing. If we step back, if we look at our arguments the way others look at them, we will begin to see the impact of our glasses. Moreover, if we take off the glasses, then we will see that the passages on praise are concerned about much more than externals. We will allow the passages to address their main points, not turn them so that they merely address our issue.

I write for several groups of people.

1) I am writing for people who grew up in non-instrumental, non-solo churches who have had difficulty comprehending our distinct rules on praise. You have wondered why some praise experiences that inspire you were not welcome "inside the building." You probably learned early on that this was a topic you were not particularly free to question. Emotions ran high.

This is also the topic that kept you from fellowship with other Christians. As you struggled with Jesus' supreme desire for unity among his followers, this topic kept you from being able to do one of the simplest things – praise God – with them, except on "Church of Christ" terms. It withheld fellowship.

It marginalized you, keeping other Christians from ever taking you seriously. They were tempted to listen to what you had to say about other topics, but doubted your ability to reason because of instruments and solos. Maybe this book will let you study privately, without fear that others will pass judgment while you're in the process.

All your life, you were taught to look at praise passages for evidence of instruments or solos, but now you can look at them for evidence of much more. Many of you have already left the Churches of Christ. Maybe this will help you to heal.

2) I am writing for my brothers and sisters who yet believe that God now opposes instruments, solos, and choruses in worship ... and who wonder why so many others disagree. Many of you play instruments; you don't hate them. You just don't see anyone taking you seriously enough to answer your questions. It hurts to feel like people are leaving you behind without even trying to discuss the issues. For many of you, your only exposure to the opposite view is what you have heard second hand from one another. There are indeed bad arguments for instruments and solos, but you have never heard the good ones. Perhaps you don't have relationship with *any* Christian outside of your fellowship that you can ask. Perhaps now someone who has sincerely tried to examine our arguments can present a differing view in a way that answers your questions. I don't blame you for your skepticism. I also know that you will be blessed by examining these praise passages with a broader expectation. I look forward to time with you.

3) I am writing for those who want to talk with their friends in the first two groups (above) on this issue. You have scratched your head and wondered why Christians would embrace the belief that God should now oppose so much that once pleased him in praise. When you've tried to discuss it, your arguments and those of your friend have seemed to be two ships passing in the night, with neither of you understanding the other's view. I pray that these pages may let you inside the mind of your friend, so that you can have a productive discussion.

4) I write for those of you who yearn for unity. My desire is that an examination of our arguments on instruments and solos can help us evaluate our standard for unity in many areas.

Again, for all of these groups, my prayer is that our study will lead us into a richer experience of praise.

As we conclude this chapter, let me introduce three paragraphs that will close out most chapters.

*Who changed praise?* That's an essential question. If our young people are to hold to our tradition of praise as a mandate from God, then they want to know where God made the mandate. We must ask who brought an end to solos and the use of instruments. At the end of most chapters, we will summarize what we have learned in search of the answer to that critical question. We will review the evidence to see who changed praise when Jesus died.

*Were you surprised?* We are going to be taking take a critical look at arguments posed by scholars on both sides of the debate. (If we in the pew are not capable of that, then we and those who differ with us are only deferring to our preferred scholars, and God is judging us on issues we are helpless to understand.) As we investigate, there will be times when the arguments of our own scholars will surprise us. We will find ourselves saying things like, "I didn't know we believed that!" Each chapter will conclude with a recap of its "blow me down" discoveries.

*Are you missing more than music?* These chapters will also conclude with a summary paragraph on removing the blinders to our praise. As we find that these passages have more to offer than an opinion on our debate, we want to experience the focus of the inspired writer. We will look at what we can do to better capture God's desire for praise and for unity in a spirit of love.

# Five Disputable Matters

*Accept him whose faith is weak, without passing judgment on disputable matters.*
- the Apostle Paul (Romans 14:1)

I am looking for a short term to define the belief that would prohibit solos, choruses, and instruments in praise to God. May I simply call it "Exclusion?"

For 100 years, Exclusion has broken fellowship over five issues regarding our worship in song. These five arguments comprise the five sections of this study. The Apostle Paul asked us to accept one another, "without passing judgment on disputable matters" (Romans 14:1). This book alleges that all five of these arguments are at best "disputable matters." They are identified briefly in this section before we begin our study. The first of the five comes from a study of history.

1.  Exclusion contends that the early church believed that God wanted them to praise him *a cappella* only. Many ministers in the Churches of Christ believe that the chant of the early church is by far the strongest argument for singing *a cappella* only. We need to ask what their chant proves. We must ask *why* they chanted.

The remaining four arguments are based in scripture rather than history. Three are based in Ephesians 5:19: "Speak to one another with psalms, hymns and spiritual songs. Sing and make music in your heart to the Lord." From that verse, here are the next three disputable matters.

2. Exclusion contends that Ephesians 5:19 specifically concerns the singing of praise during "public worship," but **_not_** in other settings like our private lives. That conclusion is essential to the argument. We must ask about the setting for Ephesians 5:19.

3. Exclusion tells us that the Greek vocabulary of this passage demands that the psalms it calls us to sing should only be sung without instruments. Does the passage teach *a cappella*?

4. Exclusion argues that Ephesians 5:19 demands that in our worship assemblies everyone must always sing together ("congregationally") – no choirs, no solos. Can that be seen in those lines?

The final argument asks how we should treat those who disagree with our conclusions regarding how we sing our praise.

5. Exclusion contends that we must separate ourselves from those whose praise allows instruments and choruses. The final section of this book will ask if separation over these issues is God's will.

Before you read Exclusion's arguments (or anyone else's), before you jump to any conclusions or to the defensive, stop and read through Ephesians 5 – the whole chapter – for yourself, from several translations. Ask yourself these questions: In context, does any translation look like Exclusion? Does any translation make Ephesians 5:19 sound *only* like an assembly? Does any translation communicate its meaning with words like "*a cappella*" or "unison"? Before you read the arguments of others, read Ephesians 5 with your own eyes.

When you're done, we'll begin with Exclusion's first disputable matter.

Exclusion's First
Disputable Matter:

"God Commanded the
Early Church to Chant."

# Why Do Scholars Disagree?

*I must say that I regard the controversy over this matter as unimportant.*
-F.W. Gingrich, co-editor of *A Greek-English Lexicon*
*of the New Testament*, 1957 and 1979 editions,
commenting on the *a cappella* question.[1]

It can be a hopeless feeling to see scholars so divided over accompaniment in praise. If they cannot agree, then what are we in the pews to do? Exclusion's scholars are respectable men, and they seem certain that we should praise God only *a cappella*. The majority of scholars, however, disagree. What is perhaps surprising is that these dissenters seem to see no point in debating it. They have not lined up to write books defending instruments. Exclusion is tempted to conclude that they do not write because their arguments are weak. To the contrary, as Gingrich points out in his quote, the sobering truth is that they think answering would be a waste of their time.

I have received the same counsel. "You're wasting your time," some have offered. "No one is going to change his mind." A few take this line of reasoning to an ominous conclusion: "We're just waiting for a generation to die."

This advice disappoints me, but I understand why so many have given up. For over 100 years we have anticipated the arrival of the latest

New Testament Greek lexicons (dictionaries), hoping that the next one will settle the dispute over accompaniment once and for all, and for over 100 years we have come away from each new volume clinging to the same differing positions we have always held. Unless we ask *why* we reach different conclusions, we are destined to entrench ourselves more deeply in the same opposing camps. Forever we will question the credibility of the scholars who have a different understanding. To escape this division, our critical need is to understand how we can look at the same lexicons and evaluate the evidence differently. We must understand what we bring to our study that prejudices us to disagree.

We are tempted to believe that people reach different conclusions because one side or the other doesn't have all of the facts. We think that if we just present our evidence to the other side, then honest people will walk away in agreement. With great expectation, we offer our arguments, yet the other side is not persuaded. If we don't understand *why* the facts look different between us, then we may begin to question the integrity, motives, intelligence, or stubbornness of those who disagree. The debate over instruments has known too many of these suspicions and hurtful accusations.

The truth of the matter is that when someone asks *why* you believe what you believe, the answer comes in two levels. On the surface level, you may think of what you consider to be the evidence for your beliefs. A deeper level considers the assumptions – perhaps unconscious – that govern what you see when you look at that evidence. If we do not know what assumptions we hold, then we will be controlled by them. We won't even realize that they are influencing our ability to examine the facts. This chapter looks at these deeper presumptions that we bring with us when we look at the evidence for worship. It offers hope that by bringing those presumptions into the light we may come to agreement.

Fortunately for us, Exclusion – the opposition to instruments and solos – tips its hand. It makes known the underlying basis of thought that directs its understanding of scripture. We can know why we look at the same evidence and disagree. There is hope for unity.

Our first stop will be to ask why the early church said it chanted. We will ask that question first because it stands alone at the center of the debate. A scholar's answer to that question accurately predicts what he will find when investigating every other question addressed by the debate. In the next chapter we will ask why the early church chanted. In this chapter, we ask what difference the answer to that question makes when we open the Bible. In the chapters that follow, we will see the influence of Exclusion's answer to that question in every disputable matter.

An example comes from Milo Hadwin as he argues for *a cappella* singing only. He observes that before the first century, Jews and pagans had used instruments when praising God, but that the early church praised God *a cappella*. From this he concludes,

*Nothing less than a command of God would have been sufficient to account for such a radical reversal in belief and practice.*[2]

Notice that his reasoning runs backwards from what one would expect. Hadwin doesn't say that the scriptures teach exclusively *a cappella* singing, and therefore that explains why the early church chanted. He rather asserts that only a command of God could explain the chant of the early church, so that's what the New Testament passages must teach. He finds a way for those passages to teach *a cappella* only, because he believes that nothing less could explain the early church chant. The scriptures don't form his conclusion; they conform to it. The presumption that the early church believed God commanded chanting is the underlying premise that directs how he interprets scripture. His premise will help us understand arguments that he makes when we consider them later in this book.

Hadwin explains up front where he is coming from and how he could understand passages differently from other scholars who allow instruments. Frequently, though, Exclusion's scholars do not seem to recognize how their belief about the early church chant influences their understanding of scripture. When they draw conclusions from scripture that seem hard to defend, it is often helpful to consider how that premise may have influenced their thinking.

Sometimes people frame this argument by saying, "I just think there is something that those first Christians understood about our singing passages that we don't understand." The thought is that as Paul traveled about, he made something clear to the early church that he never wrote down so clearly in scripture. It says that we need to deduce what Paul might have told them and then interpret the Bible to match our conclusions. It is not the style of argument you come to expect from the Churches of Christ. We would never agree to let that line of reasoning filter scripture on any other matter of faith. At its heart, it implies that the Bible is incomplete. Trying to make sense of the early church chant, we re-evaluate the scriptures. Hardly realizing we are governed by a premise – much less researching whether or not that premise is true – we work to align the scriptures with this suspicion that God – somehow – commanded the first Christians to sing *a cappella* only.

We must acknowledge that Exclusion comes by this method of evaluating scripture honestly. It stems from our commitment to interpret scriptures in harmony with one another. If I interpret a passage in a way that contradicts the clear teaching of a second passage, then I take another look at the first passage to see what I have missed. I reevaluate my understanding of the first passage so that it aligns with the second passage. Scripture must agree with scripture. The difference here is that Exclusion makes scripture harmonize not with other scriptures, but with its own interpretation of history. It tries to make scripture agree with its belief that the early church chanted by command of God. As we shall see, this leads to interpretations of scripture that are forced or puzzling.

Think for a moment about someone you know who holds a belief that you see as not based in scripture. I once knew man who thought that Christians could never drink alcohol. He said that "drinking one drop of alcohol makes you one drop drunk." When I asked about Jesus turning the water to the best wine (John 4:10), he said that the best wine wouldn't be intoxicating. When I said that Jesus admitted that he was known for drinking wine – as distinct from John the Baptist, who never drank – (Luke 7:33, 34), my acquaintance had an answer. When I offered scriptures that distinguished drinking from drunkenness (like Ephesians 5:18 and 1 Timothy 3:8), he was sure they taught that Christians couldn't drink a drop. I pointed out that God nowhere told us to abstain from wine, but that was irrelevant to him. Even the command to Timothy to, "Stop drinking only water, and use a little wine," (1 Timothy 5:23) was unpersuasive. He was certain that I had misunderstood the meanings of the Greek words. Unless I produced a passage that said "Christians may drink wine that is alcoholic," he was not going to be persuaded. His opinion led him to read scripture with a "prove me wrong" approach ... and nothing could prove him wrong. He interpreted scripture from a faulty context, a context based on a premise that was not true. He imagined that the scriptures taught what he had concluded before he opened them.

People gave up trying to persuade him otherwise. They considered it a waste of time. He could not see the scriptures in any other light. No one knew how to correct his premise.

I once looked at our scriptural basis for opposing instruments and solos and felt the same sense of hopelessness in trying to answer it. I knew it didn't matter that there is no verse to break with the Old Testament and forbid instruments. I felt that if I couldn't produce a scripture that said "Christians must praise with instruments," then Exclusion would not be persuaded. The hurdle to be overcome is the premise that the early church chanted by command of God.

In my observation, if we cannot agree about a passage on worship, then asking what we believe about why the early church chanted can help explain why. If Exclusion is correct – if God commanded the chant – then the scriptures must teach what Exclusion says. If Exclusion's premise is not certain, however, then we will begin to see how the scriptures strain to validate its conclusions. Recognizing what premise we bring to the table as we study the scriptures enables us to be aware of how that premise impacts our understanding. This realization gives us the hope that we may agree together. We are empowered to go beyond those scholars who believe that further discussion is a waste of time. We hold the key to unlocking the door that separates us.

In the next chapter, we look at why the early church chanted. In chapters that follow that, we will see how Exclusion's belief that God commanded the first century chant influences its interpretation of scripture. Repeatedly, we will see how this premise leads our scholars to stand alone.

---

[1] F.W. Gingrich, in a letter dated to April 29, 1962, *Documents on Instrumental Music,* by Tom Burgess (College Press, 1966), pp 45-46.

[2] Milo Richard Hadwin, "Chapter 4. What Kind of Music Does God Want?" Sheerer, Jim and Williams, Charles L., editors, *Directions for the Road Ahead: Stability in Change Among the Churches of Christ,* (Chickasha, Okla.: Yeoman Press, 1998), pp.55.

# Why Did the Early Church Chant?

*The immediate setting for early Christianity, the synagogue and sectarian Judaism, as we have seen, favored the practice of purely vocal music.*[1]
- Everett Ferguson, supporter of *a cappella* singing

Did you know the Jews were already singing *a cappella* when John baptized Jesus? The Bible doesn't talk about it at all. If the Bible were all you had, you would never know that the first century Jews were big chanters. If the Bible were all you had, you wouldn't know that the early church chanted either. You may want to turn those thoughts over in your mind for a moment. It's astonishing, really.

The Bible doesn't address the wide-spread, first century chant. In discussing the New Testament words for Christian singing, Exclusion's most favorable lexicon first concedes, "Although the New Testament does not voice opposition to instrumental accompaniment..,"[2] and then the author launches his discussion of history. In 1972, Exclusion's most respected scholar, Abilene Christian University's Everett Ferguson (cited above), wrote *A Cappella Music in the Public Worship of the Church.* The opening chapter is a 42-page study titled, "The New Testament Evidence." Its final paragraph begins with the words, "Before leaving the New Testament references, we may note in passing that the New Testament gives no negative judgment on instrumental music *per se.*"[3]

With that, Ferguson moves on to make his case in a lengthy chapter titled, "The Testimony of History." The Bible itself doesn't tell us that Jews and early Christians widely sang *a cappella*.

History alone tells us that the early church chanted, perhaps chanted exclusively. But that is only half of the story. The other half of the story – the half that begs to be told – is the half that tells us *why* the early church chanted. Did Christians attribute their chant to a command of God, or were they merely in step with their culture? Was the chant commanded or coincidence? Curiously, the Bible tells neither half of the story. History alone tells us *that* early Christians chanted. History alone tells us *why* they chanted.

Those who allow musical instruments in praise do not dispute that the early church chanted. That half of the story is not contested. Those who use instruments merely disagree about the other half of the story, the half that tells *why* early Christians chanted. Knowing why they chanted makes all the difference in the world.

Suppose for a moment that Exclusion is correct about why the early church chanted. If the first Christians believed that God commanded chanting, that evidence would be powerful. We would re-evaluate the lexicons and the New Testament, just as Exclusion does. Although the Bible may not seem to clearly <u>teach</u> *a cappella*, we would at least want to show that it doesn't <u>contradict</u> *a cappella*, just like Exclusion.

On the other hand, what if the early church chanted for some other reason? After all, the chanting alone is not conclusive evidence of a commandment of God. So, what if the early church never attributed their chant to God? What if their chant was motivated by cultural reasons, not by inspired ones? That would change everything, wouldn't it?

This chapter asks *why* the early church chanted. It is not merely a fair question, but a fundamental one. If the early church believed that God commanded *a cappella* praise <u>only</u>, then we should expect to see the early church cite those scriptures. On the other hand, if they acknowledge no command from God, then we would expect to uncover other reasons for their chant. This chapter asks if the early church believed that God himself commanded *a cappella* praise <u>only</u>.

Our look at history will examine four witnesses called by Exclusion: (1) the influence of the Pharisees, (2) the preference for vocal music,

(3) the condemnation of instruments outside of worship, and (4) the condemnation of David. Before we look at those arguments, let's note an argument that Exclusion's scholars do not make.

## ~~0. The Early Church Condemned Instruments in Worship~~

No one argues that the early church condemned instruments in worship. You may have thought that our scholars made that argument, but they do not. You might like to see examples, but there are none. As we shall see, the condemnation of instruments in worship begins in the fifth century, and then it condemns even David's use of instruments in praise. Before the fifth century, we see a preference for vocal music and a condemnation of instruments in settings of immorality, but there is no condemnation of instruments in worship. That's why we must scratch out this argument.

Since the early church never condemns instruments in worship, it goes without saying that they never cite any passage of scripture as opposing accompaniment in praise. The "exhibit A" argument that Exclusion would like to present does not exist. The early church never says that God condemned instruments in worship.

What does Exclusion make of this silence? Ferguson argues that the silence merely implies that instruments were not used in worship. He writes,

> *There is no polemic* [argument made] *against instruments in the church. That is not under consideration.... In view of the violent response to immoral uses of instruments in social life and their cultic use in pagan religion, it becomes incredible that the instrument was present in the worship of the church. That surely would have brought condemnation, or at least called for explanation. But there is not even a comment to this effect.*[4]

Another scholar who initially agreed with Ferguson's conclusion regarding the silence is James McKinnon. In 1987, as Professor of Music at State University of New York at Buffalo, he published, *Music in Early Christian Literature*. I found him because he is noted by those who oppose instruments. In his 1965 doctoral dissertation, he asserts that the *reason* that the early church never condemns instruments in worship to God was surely because no one ever tried to use them. He wrote,

> *Now a close reading of all the patristic criticism of instruments leads to the remarkable conclusion that there is not a single quotation which condemns the use of instruments in church: ... If it had ever occurred to any Christian communities of the third or fourth centuries to add instruments to their liturgical singing, indignation over the action would certainly be prominent in patristic literature.*[5]

It is interesting to see how this scholar changes his opinion after further study. We will take a closer look later in this chapter.

The early church never condemned instruments in worship. Before we explain the silence, we must acknowledge it. There is no "Thus saith the Lord" from the early church.

Now we are ready to look at the arguments that *are* made against instruments in praise.

## I. The Influence of the Pharisees

From Exclusion's perspective, the debate over instruments focuses a great deal on the Greek word, *psallō*. We will study it at length when we examine New Testament (Greek) words for Christian singing. *Psallō* is the verb for sing that goes with *psalmos*, the noun that gives us "psalm." As we shall see, the primary first century meaning of *psallō* was to sing with or without instruments, and it continued to be used for playing an instrument (regardless of accompanied voice) for generations after the apostles. Obviously, Exclusion does not prefer those meanings in the New Testament. Exclusion does not believe that you could sing praise to God with or without instruments.

The reason that *psallō* is central to the debate is because Exclusion sees it as the most difficult word to harmonize with its premise that the early church chanted by command of God. You see, when the Jews translated the Hebrew Old Testament into Greek, they used the Greek word "psalm" to identify the hymns of praise that used instruments.

Just as the noun "psalm" described accompanied songs, the related verb *psallō* described the act of singing with accompaniment. Although he strongly supports only *a cappella* singing, Ferguson acknowledges that in the first century "Hellenistic [Greek-speaking] Jews writing for Gentile audiences kept to the classical [instrumental] meaning of *psallō*."[6] He gives the famous Josephus as an example of a Jew writing in the common Greek of the day who always used *psallō* for instrumental music.[7] (Again, we'll look in more detail later.)

The real question for Exclusion, then, is *why* the New Testament authors would have used a word with such instrumental implications, assuming those authors opposed instruments in worship. Why would the New Testament authors *exclude* instruments with the same word?

In his lexicon, Frederick Danker addresses this dilemma. After first acknowledging the instrumental use of *psallō* in the days of the Apostles, he then argues against the thought of instruments in the New Testament. It's not what you would have expected, is it? If we become fully persuaded of the scholarly argument, we will only say that *psallō* had a more narrow usage in the New Testament than it did elsewhere in the first century. Here is Danker's quote: *"Although the New Testament does not voice opposition to instrumental accompaniment, in view of Christian opposition to mystery cults, as well as Pharisaic aversion to musical instruments in worship (s. EWerner, art. "Music", IDB 3, 466-9) it is likely that some such sense as make melody is best here* [in Eph 5:19]."[8] Let's begin with the Pharisees.

It is perhaps a surprising discovery to learn that the Pharisees had come to oppose their own temple instruments before the New Testament was written. The same opinion, however, did not overtake the Sadducees, the opposing Jewish sect that actually oversaw the temple. For an understanding of the history, Danker points to an article in *The Interpreter's Dictionary of the Bible*. Regarding musical instruments, the article's author (E. Werner) contends that the Apostles also didn't like instruments. In this sense, Werner says that the apostles were "in accord with the Pharisees, opposed to the ruling class of the Sadducees, who dominated the temple." Werner sees evidence of this opposition to instruments in Paul's mention of them in 1 Corinthians 13:1 ("… a resounding gong or a clanging cymbal"):

*Explicitly stated here is the primacy of vocal music over any instrumental music. Implicit is the contempt of all instrumental music, and the emphatic disparagement of "gong" (χαλκοσ) and cymbals, two of the temple's percussion instruments. This sentiment was vastly different from the Gentile attitude, which favored these instruments. Paul, however, denounced their usage on account of their role in the mystery cults, and thus reflected the views of the orthodox Pharisees as well as some ideas of Philo's philosophy.*
*Paul, himself a "Pharisee of Pharisees," shared fully these views....*[9]

Later, Werner adds:

*However the Pharisees might have felt about the temple orchestra, which was exclusively in Saducean hands, banquet music was welcome in their houses.*[10]

How interesting it is that the first century Pharisees opposed instruments in the same settings that Exclusion does today! They welcomed instruments in their homes and opposed them in public worship. Werner believes that these Pharisees influenced the Apostles to do the same. A more interesting question may be to ask who influenced the Pharisees. They certainly were not influenced by God. There was no Old Testament command to "disparage" the temple instruments. This is not surprising, for Jesus said the Pharisees had a habit of setting aside God's commands in favor of their own (Mark 7:5-8). Exclusion has argued that only a command of God could explain a change to *a cappella* singing, but here we see that the Pharisees were quite capable of the change all by themselves.

Werner argues that the Apostle Paul "reflected the views of the orthodox Pharisees as well as some ideas of Philo's philosophy." Werner says that Paul was influenced by the culture of his day to oppose instruments in worship. Now, this Philo that Werner references was a first century (non-Christian) Jewish philosopher. Ferguson writes, "Philo's extensive writings permit us to gain a full picture of the way Jewish religious and Greek philosophical thought on the subject of music flowed together at the beginning of the Christian era."[11] Indeed, we find that there *were* cultural influences in the first century. Ferguson cites examples where Philo praises vocal music, opposes instruments "to arouse lust," and promotes "the concept of 'silent singing' as the highest type of praise."[12] This "Jewish religious and Greek philosophical thought" was not born of a command from God.

Danker's argument is that the New Testament writers may have used *psallō* exclusively in a sense that excluded instruments, distinct from other writers of their day. He explicitly says that his argument is based on contemporary, cultural influences opposing instruments. These influences could explain why early Christians might have preferred vocal singing, though they never said that God opposed instruments. To the contrary, Revelation 15:2, 3 (*"They held harps given them by God and sang the song of Moses the servant of God and the song of the lamb"*) doesn't sound like the Apostle John was "in accord with the Pharisees" or the culture of his day in opposition to musical instruments in worship. It rather sounds like this apostle was in accord with God. The Pharisees' opposition to a command of God was *never* enough to *change* a command of God, but often enough to *disobey* it. I have difficulty concluding that the Apostles were influenced by the Pharisees to oppose instruments in worship. The apostles never spoke out against instruments; the Pharisees did.

Perhaps the greatest failing of this argument is that no early Christian ever suggests that they chanted because of the meaning of *psallō*. You see, it's not enough to merely say that in the first century *psallō* allowed *a cappella* singing (which it did). All of the Greek singing verbs allow *a cappella*. The question is if the first century Christians thought that *psallō* demanded *a cappella* singing only. They never said so. Excluding instruments based on the meaning of the word *psallō* is a modern argument that never seems to have occurred to the chanting early church.

Danker's arguments for preferring a restricted meaning for *psallō* in the New Testament may be contrasted with the observation of his one-time co-editor F. W. Gingrich. "It seems to me that you cannot exclude the possibility of accompaniment in the N.T. passages, since ψαλλο [*psallō*] still means 'play on the harp' in Lucian, who wrote in the second century A.D."[13]

## 2. The Preference for Vocal Music

There is plenty of evidence that the early church chanted. This put them in step with the culture of their day. Ferguson writes, "The immediate setting for early Christianity, the synagogue and sectarian Judaism, as we have seen, favored the practice of purely vocal music."[14] So strong was this cultural influence of the day that Ferguson later adds, "Although it would be bold to say that an instrument was never used by Christians in their public assemblies, I can say that if it was, it was exceptional and unusual."[15] We find the preference for vocal singing, but no statement that *God* opposed instruments in worship. An example is an early Christian named Clement, who wrote around the turn of the third century (200 A.D.). Ferguson shares this quote from Clement:

> *The one instrument of peace, the Word alone by which we honour God, is what we employ. We no longer employ the ancient psaltery, the trumpet, and timbrel, and flute, which those expert in war and contemners of the fear of God were wont to make use of also in the choruses at their festive assemblies; that by such strains they might raise their dejected minds."[16]*

Clement tells us his practice, but he falls short of saying that "God said" not to use instruments. To the contrary, elsewhere he writes,

> *The Lord is now our congenial guest, for the Apostle adds again, 'teaching and admonishing one another in all wisdom, singing psalms, hymns, and spiritual songs with thankfulness in your hearts to God. And whatsoever you do, in word or deed, do everything in the name of the Lord Jesus, giving thanks to God the father through him.' (Col 3.16-17) This is our grateful revelry, and if you should wish to sing and play to the cithara and lyre, this is not blameworthy; you would imitate the just Hebrew king giving praise to God. 'Rejoice in the Lord, O you righteous! Praise befits the upright' (Ps 32:1) says the prophecy. 'Praise the Lord on the cithara, make melody to him on the psaltery of ten strings! Sing to him a new song' (Ps 32.2)[17]*

Ferguson, who favors *a cappella* worship only, makes some interesting comments about Clement. Regarding this last quotation, Ferguson believes that Clement perhaps allows psalms to be sung to an instrument at home.[18] Later, he adds, "It should further be noted that Clement's statement concerns what is done at a banquet in the home, not at a church service nor even at an agapē (love feast)."[19] Clement's quote about accompanied worship is made to conform to Exclusion's premise that the early church chanted by command of God. The unseen premise demands that we deduce some explanation for Clement's acceptance of accompaniment in praise. To meet this need, Ferguson infers permission for them in worship at home only. However, if Clement believed that God condemned the use of instruments in praise, it is hard to argue that he would condone them anyway in certain worship contexts. Furthermore, the Biblical citations that Clement makes do not easily lend themselves to restricted settings. Reread Clement's quote, and see if you see the influence of the premise in Ferguson's evaluation.

Ferguson's other interesting comment regards Clement's "allegorical interpretation" of the instruments in the Old Testament: "Clement seems to have taken his cue from Philo. As Philo, he compares man, composed of body and soul and like a miniature universe, to an instrument."[20] Once again, we find reference that the early church is listening to uninspired Jewish philosophy. In the church's view of music, we find a strong influence from the world. We do not find a condemnation of accompanied praise as though it were from God. We must speak clearly. We rather find opinion to the contrary.

## 3. The Condemnation of Instruments Outside of Worship

Early Christians preferred vocal music, but they condemned instruments *outside of* worship. A modern authority on music in the early church is James McKinnon. In 1987, as Professor of Music at State University of New York at Buffalo, he published, *Music in Early Christian Literature*. Years earlier, as a doctoral student, he had agreed with Ferguson that Christians would have condemned instruments in the church if anyone had tried to use one. We saw his quote earlier in this chapter. Another two decades of study changed his mind. Here is what he has to say as a seasoned professor.

A. **Written opposition (from the church fathers) to *any* instruments in *any* setting was born in the third century, almost 200 years after Jesus.**[21] (Again, the opposition was outside of Christian worship.) McKinnon wonders why the opposition to instruments "should have been absent from the writings of earlier church fathers and so prominent in those of later ones."[22] He suggests that the truth may be quite different from what Werner (above) suggested; he does not suppose that the Pharisees influenced the apostles. Instead, he suspects that it was these later church fathers that were influenced by the world in their new-found opposition to instruments: "The later fathers on the other hand, all thoroughly educated in the classical tradition, might be said to have shared the musical Puritanism of pagan intellectuals, taking it – for reasons of their own – beyond all precedent."[23] Opposition in the third century was *new*. Once again we find a scholar citing the influence of the world regarding a change in the church.

B. **Opposition to instruments was not blanket, but limited to their role in contexts of immorality.** Yes, the church opposed "pagan musical practice with pagan cults."[24] But the church's opposition to instruments was "at least as strong" in a "limited number" of contexts of sexual immorality. McKinnon writes, "Typically singled out are items of moral concern like the lewd aspect of theatrical musicians, the coarseness of marriage songs and the dubious profession of female musicians employed at banquets."[25] Blaming the instruments in these contexts was something new. Ferguson similarly speaks of "ancient church fathers, who go beyond the New Testament in pronouncing a negative judgment on musical instruments. They give an explicit condemnation to instrumental music."[26]

C. **At the same time, the early church frequently wrote of instruments in a *positive* light.** These same early church authors accepted music as a liberal art and frequently made musical illustrations. (A musical illustration would be on the order of saying that Christians work together with one purpose, even as the many strings of a harp work together to produce a song.) In fact, instrumental illustrations occur far more frequently in Christian writings than any other musical texts in the first three centuries.[27] Remember that Ferguson said that Clement was taking "his cue" from the first century philosopher Philo when he wrote in this way.

D. **Opposition to pagan instruments was unrelated to music in the church.** McKinnon found no correlation between the "liturgical chant" of the early church and the opposition to instruments in other contexts. He writes,

> *"[W]hat relationship is there between the polemic* [the argument] *against instruments and the a cappella performance of sacred music? Music historians have tended to assume that there is a direct connection, that is, that ecclesiastical* [church] *authorities consciously strove to maintain their music free from the incursion of musical instruments. There is little evidence of this in the sources however.*[28]

McKinnon removed himself from the instrumental music dispute. He followed the lead of the church fathers, who he said had left this debate "to the *a cappella* partisans of the nineteenth century."[29]

Another important observation of McKinnon regards *when* Christians sang. Having studied the scant material available from second and third century writers, McKinnon found that Christians primarily sang together in their homes, with little discussion of singing in their assemblies. [30]

Exclusion faces two dilemmas.

1. Dilemma #1: **the "just-don't-call-it-worship" loophole:** Did early Christians intend for us to deduce rules for assemblies *only* (exempting our daily, "private" lives) based on their writings about daily life?

- Did the church fathers intend to forbid singing a song, maybe one you have written, to Christians in your home? If not, could you do the same in an assembly?

- Did the church fathers intend to forbid clapping or physical motions in children's songs in your home (or during VBS)? If not, could you do the same in an assembly?

- Did the church fathers intend to forbid a group singing to a shut-in brother or sister? If not, could a choir sing in an assembly?

- Did the church fathers intend to forbid the use of instruments in any song where God's name is praised? ...in your home? ...in weddings or funerals? ...at Christmas? ...on a tape or on the radio? ...in learning or writing a song? If not, could instruments be heard in an assembly?

2. Dilemma #2: **binding what is not written:** Shall we make binding rules based on what early Christians did not say?

McKinnon observes, "The typical early Christian reference to music is an incidental remark made by a church father in some lengthy work on an entirely different subject."[31] Exclusion puts these pieces together as a puzzle to deduce a foundational command never mentioned on any piece. If the church fathers opposed accompaniment in worship in either the home or in "designated assemblies," it is odd that they *never said so.* Neither the Bible nor the early church for several hundred years speaks a word against accompaniment in Christian worship. Acceptance of Christians singing with accompaniment would not contradict the writings of any church father until the dawn of the fifth century.

Exclusion answers "yes" to these dilemmas through the prism of its premise that the early church chanted by command of God.

# 4. The Condemnation of David

Opposition to instruments in worship did arise in some later church fathers. Particularly noted are fifth century Christians of the school of Antioch, figures like John Chrysostom and Theodoret of Cyrus (who died around 457 A.D.). These later Christians are cited by both McKinnon and Ferguson. It is true that these authors began condemning instruments in worship, but they also condemned instruments in the hands of David. They said that God never *enjoyed* instruments even under the old law, but had allowed this "evil" for a time in an effort to wean his people away from idol worship. I was amazed when I read this quote from Theodoret.

> *Of old the Levites used these instruments as they hymned God in his holy Temple, not because God enjoyed their sound but because he accepted the intention of those involved. We hear God saying to the Jews that he does not take pleasure in singing and playing: 'Take away from me the sound of your songs; to the voice of your instruments I will not listen' (Amos 5.23). He allowed these things to happen because he wished to free the Jews from the error of idols. For since they were fond of play and laughter, and all these things took place in the temple of the idols, he permitted them ... thus avoiding the greater evil by allowing the lesser.*[32]

As we know, the inspired word never gives a hint of this alleged motive of God for instruments. (We don't get the impression that David needed to be weaned away from idolatrous instruments.) Theodoret was clearly trying to spin the Old Testament in a light that agreed with his *a cappella* beliefs. McKinnon finds that this "lesser evil" argument is "expanded and repeated" by other authors of Antioch.[33]

The weight that Ferguson places on these fifth century authors is surprising to me. He writes,

> *The conclusion that the early church did not employ instrumental music in worship does not rest, however, on inferences from silence. There are explicit statements from early Christian writers to the effect that Christians did not use instrumental music. ...Statements written near*

36

*the year 400 from both the Greek and Latin halves of Christendom declare the absence of instrumental music in Christian worship.*[34]

Ferguson's first quote to support this view is from Theodoret, and he even goes on to cite the example given here. He calls attention to Chrysostum and the school of Antioch, but summarizes their teaching in a somewhat harmless light: "God allowed the Jews to use instrumental music, even as he allowed animal sacrifice, not because that was what he desired, but as a transitional practice of leading the people from idolatry to true spiritual worship."[35] These fifth century writers call the instruments that God asked for "evil." That is so far from Biblical truth that I cannot see them as an authority for how I should sing today. Can you? (As we shall discuss later, modern Exclusion calls instruments "unspiritual" rather than "evil.")

About this same time, a bishop named Niceta also wrote on the topic of music. Ferguson notes that, "He opposed the interpretation of those few who advocated "silent singing" in the church and explained David's harp as a symbol of the cross of Christ."[36] Still, centuries later, we see the lingering influence of first century, non-Christian philosophy upon the church.

Ferguson's quote here began by saying that instruments were excluded by "inferences from silence" until the dawn of the fifth century. The statement is curious, because we have seen that history is not silent. We have already seen examples from Clement and Lucian. Tom Burgess cites numerous others in chapter 6 of his *Documents on Instrumental Music.*[37] We will continue to see Exclusion dismiss citations that favor instruments and then exclude instruments based on the remaining silence. Until the fifth century, there is silence if we look for the condemnation of instruments in worship. This chapter opened with that confession from Exclusion's scholars. In contrast to that silence, history has spoken in support of instruments.

What have we learned from our study of history?

If we are to find a written *"a cappella"* mandate from the early church, then we must hurdle centuries of writings that never oppose accompaniment in praise, though they oppose it in settings of immorality. We must limit the scope of statements that *allow* accompaniment in praise so that they only apply to "private" worship.

We must take up the mantel of fifth century Christians without being tainted by their equal opposition to the instruments of David's day. Perhaps this explains why we have had had such difficulty getting the Biblical passages to fit the "*a cappella* only" mold.

Better said, if there is no mandate, then we are free to re-examine the Biblical passages. We don't have to believe that the Apostles "reflected" the Pharisees' rebellious opposition to instruments. We don't have to say that *psallō* had a different meaning in the New Testament than it did everywhere else in the first century. We don't have to say that passages about our daily lives contain rules for singing praise in our assemblies that don't apply to our "private" lives (chapters 6 and 7 of this book). We are released from trying to explain how Paul commanded <u>*only*</u> *a cappella* singing with the same words that John repeatedly used of singing God's praise *with* accompaniment (chapter 9). When David praises God among the nations with instruments in a prophecy for our day, we don't have to be embarrassed about the citation (chapter 10). We don't have to label David as the father of "unspiritual" (or "lesser of two evils") praise (chapter 11). We don't have to say that the only explanation for the early church's chant is a mandate from God that they never produce.

If we step back from Exclusion's premise that only a command of God could explain the first century chant, then we can look at history and the scriptures with a new set of eyes. We can take off the "*a cappella*-colored glasses!"

Before this chapter closes, I must add a few words of commendation for Everett Ferguson. Again, this gentleman is recognized by many as the leading scholar of our generation in support of praising God *a cappella* only. I come down on the opposite side of the issue from him, but I hope to be like him in the caliber of man that he demonstrates himself to be.

In an often heated debate, I find that Ferguson always treats the people and the issues with respect. Another man with his same credentials might have been tempted to speak condescendingly to his opponents, but Ferguson speaks with grace. A man who loves winning a debate over knowing the truth might have attempted to conceal facts that were troubling to his viewpoint, but Ferguson airs them honestly. I believe I understand why we disagree, and I pray I can explain myself in this book as gracefully as he. I pray that I know my place as well as he knows his.

I have never met Everett Ferguson, but if you should mention my book to him (or to his family), then I hope you will convey the high regard that I hold for him.

**Were you surprised?** I was surprised to learn that the early church did not condemn instruments in worship, much less say that *God* opposed instruments in worship. I did not know that the third century Christians who first opposed instruments at all (in settings of immorality) were actually in step with non-Christian authors of their day. I had always heard that the reason Christians first condemned instruments in worship in the 5th century was because "that was when some Christians introduced them." No one ever mentioned to me that those same critics also passed judgment on the instruments of David's day, calling them "evil." I was amazed that 1st century Pharisees condemned instruments just like Exclusion – in public worship but not in their homes. I didn't know that Exclusion admitted that *psallō* was used differently in common Greek outside of the New Testament.

**Who changed praise?** The Pharisees tried to change Jewish praise, but failed. Did they only succeed in influencing the Apostles to oppose instruments in Christian songs? The scholarship that supports Exclusion makes this argument. Did the Pharisees influence our praise?

Some Church of Christ preachers say that *psallō* only embraced instruments in Classical Greek, not common Greek. As we shall see, no lexicon makes that case. Did acceptance of this error change praise?

The first Christians to oppose instruments at all opposed them only in limited contexts, beginning in the third century. If they are our pattern, we should oppose instruments when they did (in contexts of immorality), rather than only when they didn't (in the church).

The first Christians to write of their opposition to instruments in Christian song lived in the fifth century, some 300 years after the New Testament was completed. Theodoret and those who followed him would have stripped the instruments from David's day as well, calling them "evil." Are we changing praise for them?

Which of these is the legitimate candidate chosen by God to communicate his opposition to instruments only in worship? If there is a different messenger than we have seen, then there should be scholarly support.

The assertion that only a command of God could explain the chant of the early church is clearly disputable. God forbids that we pass judgment against those who disagree.

***Are you missing more than music?*** Our praise cannot be limited to the songs of our grandparents. Our youth do not have experience with sheaves and lighthouses. They are moved by modern melodies and modern lyrics and modern life. Their praise cannot be shackled by the preferences of the last generation. Neither can our praise be reduced to the preferences of fifth-century Christians who condemned David. Perhaps most of all, we cannot quarantine ourselves from Christians whose preferences differ from our own. It is time to embrace ceaseless praise as God commanded. Those first century Pharisees had no word from God. Still today, it is Jesus who has all authority, not them.

---

[1] Everett Ferguson, *A Cappella Music in the Public Worship of the Church (Revised Edition)*, Abilene, TX: Biblical Research Press, 1972, p. 47.

[2] Frederick William Danker, editor, *A Greek-English Lexicon of the New Testament and other Early Christian Literature*, third edition (based on Walter Bauer's sixth edition), (Chicago: University of Chicago Press, 2000), p. 1096.

[3] Ferguson, p. 42.

[4] Ferguson, p. 74.

[5] James McKinnon, *The Church Fathers and Musical Instruments*, Ph.D. diss., Columbia University, 1965 (Ann Arbor, Mich,: University Microfilms, Inc., 1967) p. 262, as found in Jim Sheerer and Charles L. Williams, editors, *Directions for the Road Ahead: Stability in Change Among the Churches of Christ*, Chickasha, OK: Yeoman Press, 1998, p. 262.

[6] Ferguson, p. 11.

[7] Ferguson, p. 11

[8] Danker, p. 1096.

[9] E. Werner, "Music," *Interpreter's Dictionary of the Bible* (Nashville, TN: Abingdon Press, 1984), p. 466.

[10] Werner, p. 468.

[11] Ferguson, p.39.

[12] Ferguson, pp. 39, 40.

[13] F.W. Gingrich, in a letter dated to April 29, 1962, *Documents on Instrumental Music*, by Tom Burgess (College Press, 1966), pp 45-46.

[14] Ferguson, p. 47.

[15] Ferguson, p. 53.

[16] Ferguson, pp. 21, 22.

[17] James McKinnon, *Music in Early Christian Literature* (Cambridge: Cambridge University Press, 1987), p.34, 35.

[18] Ferguson, p. 22.

[19] Ferguson, p. 64.

[20] Ferguson, p. 21.

[21] Speaking of the Western church fathers of the third and fourth centuries, McKinnon writes, "What they share with their Eastern counterparts [the *Greek* authors of the third century] is an awakening mistrust of pagan instrumental music." [McKinnon, p. 42]

[22] McKinnon, p. 2.

[23] McKinnon, pp. 2, 3.

[24] McKinnon, p. 3.

[25] McKinnon, p. 3.

[26] Ferguson, p. 74.

[27] McKinnon, p.5

[28] McKinnon, p. 3.

[29] McKinnon, p. 4.

[30] McKinnon, p. 9.

[31] McKinnon, p. vii.

[32] McKinnon, p. 7.

[33] McKinnon, p. 7.

[34] Ferguson, pp. 52, 53.

[35] Ferguson, p. 54.

[36] Ferguson, p. 53.

[37] Burgess, pp. 97-114.

Exclusion's Second
Disputable Matter:

"Texts on 'Worship'
Only Apply to Christian Assemblies"

# The "Just Don't Call It Worship" Loophole
# Part 1: Do verses on singing praise apply to our "private" lives?

There is just something special about Vacation Bible School, especially the songs. I love the faces of the children as they sing and shout and make hand motions or spin around or stand up and sit down or stomp their feet and clap their hands, all in songs that teach them about God.

Now here's the mystery. Clapping, choreography and shouting are not mentioned in the English New Testament. You don't see any of those words in praise passages like Ephesians 5:19 or Colossians 3:16. Those verses just tell us to sing. But Exclusion embraces VBS, where the children sing and clap and dance, and it's okay.

This chapter is *not* about whether solos, choruses, instruments, or clapping are acceptable in praise. We will look at those important questions in later chapters. Instead, this chapter is about whether the rules for singing God's praise apply *every* time we praise him, or whether there are exceptions or loopholes.

Of all the arguments about songs of praise, this one – far more than any other – exposes the gulf between those in the Churches of Christ who oppose instruments or solos and those who do not. On the one hand, our adult children cannot grasp how God's rules for praise can have such different applications on Sundays from what they have in most other settings of praise, like VBS, weddings, funerals, concerts, the radio, and singing to shut-ins. They don't see their fathers practicing what they preach. For them, this is *the most fundamental* question.

The generation of my fathers, on the other hand, appears to side step this seeming inconsistency in our songs of praise. They want to move on to Greek words and their meanings, and they seem unable to understand why their children cannot hear them when they do. They talk of exclusive rules for "public worship of the church," but their children do not understand the distinction.

These young adults don't understand why VBS isn't "pubic worship" or how funerals and weddings are "public worship" only if the prayers and songs are offered in "our" buildings. They are stunned that God's name may be praised in song with instruments if it's labeled "entertainment" (as with secular radio, shows, or concerts)[1], and wonder how others resist worshipping God at those times. They scratch their heads because so many who oppose instruments in "the public worship of the church" will sing or learn songs of praise with an instrument at home. They wonder why Christian colleges even *have* choirs, and why those choirs can sing to us after the closing prayer, but not before it. They wonder why the youth can sing to shut-ins, but not to the church.

If you are still having trouble understanding the difference, perhaps a look back in time will help. In the 1970's, many of our churches were struggling with whether or not women could wear pants instead of skirts. Those who opposed pants appealed to Deuteronomy 22:5: *"A woman must not wear men's clothing, nor a man wear women's clothing, for the LORD your God detests anyone who does this."* In time, the anti-pants lobby lost the argument because of the arbitrary way that they themselves applied this scripture. You see, the flock looked at the passage and concluded that if God "detested" pants on women, then he must detest them *all* the time.

In contrast, our shepherds selectively applied God's opposition. They publicly ruled that girls could wear shorts under their skirts for school recess, concluding that women could wear men's clothes if they wore women's clothes over them. They said that women could wear shorts or sweat pants in settings where only women were present, concluding that women weren't wearing men's clothing if no men saw them. At first, our leaders denounced the practice of women wearing pant suits to work. When women wore them anyway, our leaders bent the rules some more. Women wore pants on weekdays and taught Sunday school in skirts on Sundays. In time, many church leaders came to draw the line on pants only "in church." The system of rules for when women could and couldn't wear pants, sweat suits, and shorts became cumbersome and indefensible. *People couldn't hear the interpretation of Deuteronomy 22:5 against women's pants because those who championed opposition had a system of loopholes for breaking their own rules.* Eventually, our leaders decided that they had misunderstood the scripture to begin with. Christian women wear pants today without a second thought.

In the same way, we cannot ignore what today's younger generation rejects as a sort of "just don't call it worship" loophole. The loophole is real, and it comes from two misunderstandings. In this chapter, we will look at the misunderstanding that alleges that the New Testament verses on singing address only Christian assemblies ("public worship") as distinct from the singing of praise in most other areas of our daily lives. In the next chapter, we will look at a misunderstanding of what the New Testament identifies as "worship." In both chapters, we must ask if God expects us to be consistent in the way we apply what He asks of us when we worship him in song. We will look at praise in a new light, one that encompasses all of our lives, not just our assembled times.

## Biblical Texts on Christian Song

When a friend learns that you attend a Church of Christ, his first comment may be, "Aren't you the ones who don't believe in instruments?"

A typical response from us would be that "we aren't opposed to instruments *per se*. Indeed, many of us *play* instruments ourselves. We are opposed to instruments [and clapping, solos, and choruses] *only* in the 'public worship of the church.'" This answer is misleading in that it leaves our friends with the mistaken impression that our opposition applies to *all* songs that praise God in any way at any time. As we know, this is not the case. Before we look at Exclusion's scholarly arguments – arguments which distinguish the "public worship of the church" from songs of praise at other times – let's review New Testament passages on praise to see if *they* make such a distinction. Let's look to see if the inspired writers were addressing only limited, "designated assemblies" when they wrote about our songs of praise.

> [15]*Be very careful, then, how you live--not as unwise but as wise,* [16]*making the most of every opportunity, because the days are evil.* [17]*Therefore do not be foolish, but understand what the Lord's will is.* [18]*Do not get drunk on wine, which leads to debauchery. Instead, be filled with the Spirit.* [19]*Speak to one another with psalms, hymns and spiritual songs. Sing and make music in your heart to the Lord,* [20]*always giving thanks to God the Father for everything, in the name of our Lord Jesus Christ.* (Ephesians 5:15-20).

> [12]*Therefore, as God's chosen people, holy and dearly loved, clothe yourselves with compassion, kindness, humility, gentleness and patience.* [13]*Bear with each other and forgive whatever grievances you may have against one another. Forgive as the Lord forgave you.* [14]*And over all these virtues put on love, which binds them all together in perfect unity.* [15]*Let the peace of Christ rule in your hearts, since as members of one body you were called to peace. And be thankful.* [16]*Let the word of Christ dwell in you richly as you teach and admonish one another with all wisdom, and as you sing psalms, hymns and spiritual songs with gratitude in your hearts to God.* [17]*And whatever you do, whether in word or deed, do it all in the name of the Lord Jesus, giving thanks to God the Father through him.* (Colossians 3:12-17).

There is no doubt, is there? These paragraphs address the way we live *all* the time. Of all the New Testament passages that touch our singing, only one (I Corinthians 14: 15, 26) specifically speaks to our assemblies. All of the others are in contexts of our daily lives, addressing our singing at any time, whether with other Christians, among the lost, or alone. Bible translators give these passages headings like *Living as Children of Light* and *Rules for Holy Living*. No area of our lives is exempt.

It is impossible to say that these sections of scripture only apply to assemblies and *not* to our daily lives. Therefore, Exclusion argues that their singing verses *alone* only apply to assemblies. The "just don't call it worship" loophole relies on applying only one verse out of each chapter to "public worship" alone while conceding that all of the verses before and after apply to our daily lives. Let's take a look.

## Establishing the Loophole

Perhaps the best-known modern voice of Exclusion has been Everett Ferguson. This Abilene Christian University professor emeritus is respected for his scholarship on the practices of the early church. In 1972, he published *A Cappella Music in the Public Worship of the Church*. In it, he outlines why he believes that these singing verses only apply to "public worship," but not to our "private" lives. Other supporters of Exclusion echo his arguments.

The evidence that Ephesians 5:19 and Colossians 3:16 apply to *all* of our lives is so overwhelming that Ferguson at first concedes, "some have questioned whether these verses apply to the assembly of the church."[2] Later in the same paragraph, however, Ferguson is not merely certain that they apply to assemblies, but that they apply *only* to assemblies. Of these two verses, he concludes, "it is not a private religious exercise which is described."[3] Passages on our daily lives are found to have singing verses that must not apply to our "private" lives.

Put another way, Ferguson first argues that Ephesians 5:19 and Colossians 3:16 *also* apply to assemblies, and then makes a subtle (but huge) leap to the conclusion that they *only* apply to assemblies. Let's look at his arguments to see if they warrant the leap.

- Does the phrase "one another" imply an assembly? That's what Ferguson sees.[4] But look at how the New Testament uses "one another."[5] Yes, "one another" activity can happen in an assembly, but we cannot make the leap to say that it *only* refers to an assembly.

- Does the phrase "among you" imply an assembly? Colossians 3:16 uses a Greek phrase *"en umin,"* which is used in the New Testament for "among you, in you, with you, about you." Ferguson thinks it sounds like an assembly.[6] But see for yourself how Paul uses it. Examine these verses to see if *"en umin"* implies a public assembly, *to the exclusion of the daily life of Christians.* If the phrase implies an assembly (as Ferguson alleges), then you should see no difference if you insert the phrase "during your assemblies" in these verses.

  Romans 1:12, 13; 8:9, 10, 11; 12:3; 1 Corinthians 1:6, 10, 11; 2:22; 3:3, 16, 18; 5:1; 6:5, 19; 11:13, 18, 19, 30; 14:25; 15:12; 2 Corinthians 1:19; 4:12; 7:16; 10:1; 12:12; 13:3, 5; Galatians 3:5, 4:19, 20; Ephesians 5:3; Philippians 1:6; 2:5, 13; Colossians 1:6, 27; 3:16; 4:16; 1 Thessalonians 1:5; 2:13; 5:12; 2 Thessalonians 1:12; 3:7, 11.

  "Among you" *never* <u>implies</u> an assembly. In 1 Corinthians 11:18, Paul uses the phrase "when you come together as a church," because "among you" alone in that verse was not able to communicate the thought of an assembly. Later in that chapter, even in that assembly context, verse 30 does not mean that those who are weak and sick "among you" are only weak and sick (or asleep) during the public assembly. Again, "among you" may include an assembly, but we cannot make the leap to say that it refers *only* to an assembly. Like "one another," the phrase is typically used outside of the context of an assembly.

- Does the drunkenness of Ephesians 5:18 <u>only</u> imply worship at the temple of an idol? Ferguson says that the "drunkenness and immorality" of 5:18 is a reference to pagan worship, and that in verses 18 and 19 Paul is only making a contrast between the two worship assemblies – pagan versus Christian.[7] But such immorality was not isolated to pagan religious assemblies. It was rampant, most notably in theater, marriage celebrations, and banquets.[8] Verse 18, like 19 and the rest of the surrounding context, addresses our daily lives. We are *never* to get drunk, not even in our *"private"* lives (nor in "private worship").

• Does the singing itself imply an assembly? Ferguson contends that the teaching and singing define an assembly.[9] In my experience, teaching and singing are not limited to Sunday assemblies.

Again, on the basis of these arguments, Ferguson concludes, "In any case, it is not a private religious exercise which is described."[10] In his mind, Eph. 5:19 or Col. 3:16 do not apply to our "private" lives, but rather only to our assemblies. As we have seen, however, there is nothing in the text of those verses to justify making them apply *only* to "public worship" while all of the surrounding verses apply to our daily lives. The only justification for lifting those verses alone from their daily life contexts and limiting them to "public worship" is so that one may have a loophole for the singing of praise in our daily lives.

## Who Needs the Loophole?

One of the early Christians whose writings have come down to us was a man named Clement. As we saw in the last chapter, Ferguson deflects an awkward pro-instrument statement made by Clement with, "And this may be the precise emphasis here – one can sing even psalms to an instrument at home."[11]

Why would Exclusion argue that it was okay for Clement to praise God with instruments at home? Again we return to Exclusion's premise that the early church chanted by command of God. If there is a command to sing only *a cappella*, then the command must be in the Bible. Specifically, the command must be in Ephesians 5:19 and Colossians 3:16. The dilemma is in having those verses prohibit accompaniment in praise while allowing Clement to endorse accompaniment in praise. If one argues that the scriptures teach us to praise only *a cappella* in all settings, then Clement could not praise God with an instrument at home. Exclusion resolves the dilemma by deducing that these praise scriptures must only apply to "public" worship and that Clement must be talking only about "private" worship.

Exclusion is therefore forced to conclude that passages on a Christian's daily life include single verses about praise that must only apply to assemblies. This is why Ferguson's book is titled, "*A Cappella* Music in the Public Worship of the Church" instead of "*A Cappella* Worship." In order to accommodate writings of the early church, as well as our practices in Vacation Bible School and singing to shut-ins and listening to songs on the radio, etc., Exclusion argues that our songs of praise outside of an assembly are somewhat exempt from the New Testament passages that bind our praise during assemblies.

## What God "Didn't Have to Say"

Before we proceed, it is important here to note (again) that the impact of Exclusion's premise demonstrates itself in a variety of shades of *a cappella*-colored glasses. Though most people strive to be consistent in their application, still there will be a variety of judgments on how much choreography can occur in VBS, or how one might attend weddings or funerals not held at a Church of Christ, or whether you can listen to songs on the radio if God's name is mentioned, or why a small group can sing to shut-ins, etc. Why is there such variety? For those who practice Exclusion, the question is not *if* they use the loophole, but *when* they use the loophole. Take song teaching for example. Solos and choruses are forbidden by Exclusion, but there "must be" a scenario for teaching songs. The only question is *when* to use the loophole, when to say that the rule can be broken. For some, the loophole is that songs must be taught "outside of worship," while others make song teaching the exception to the rule against solos and choruses during assemblies.[12] Everyone sees an exemption for doing it some way. Exclusion always sees a loophole.

At this point, you might be saying that this is *ridiculous*. You may be saying that God "didn't have to say" that it is okay to respectfully attend a funeral or to teach a song or to let children make hand and body motions in their songs. If so, you have found the difference between the shades of the *a cappella*-colored glasses. The variety comes from what each one thinks that God "didn't have to say." Because God never explicitly condemned solos or instruments, because he never says *why* he would oppose them, each person must determine how to apply those rules for himself. He searches for the "mind of Christ," and determines the exceptions that he believes God "didn't have to say."

If instead our views were based on what God "did say," then we would not have such variety among ourselves in how we apply the rules. But everyone who keeps Exclusion's rules makes exceptions to those rules. The variety among us comes in what each thinks God "didn't have to say." Each of us must ask, "What do I believe God 'didn't have to say'?"

## Where Are the Rules for "Other Songs" of Praise?

If the New Testament passages on our praise aren't binding outside of our "corporate worship," then what governs that praise? Nothing. There is then no verse allowing Clement or us to use instruments in praise at home. There is then no verse allowing choruses on Sundays "after worship." There is then no verse allowing soloists to praise God at weddings or funerals. There is then no verse allowing clapping or choreography in VBS. There is then no verse allowing solos in song teaching. There is then no verse that allows you to listen to "Butterfly Kisses" on the radio. Amazingly, all of those settings are argued to be exempt from God's New Testament commands for our praise. Exclusion chastises Liberty for alleged "unauthorized" instruments and solos and the like in assemblies, and then Exclusion condones the same in praise "outside of worship" – and that, without a single verse.

What God expects of our praise to him applies whenever we praise him. There is no "just don't call it worship" loophole.

As you start to grasp the depths of Exclusion's error on this point, at the same time you begin to see the blessings that Exclusion misses in a Christian's daily life. If the true context of these passages is our daily lives – not just assemblies – then these verses address the *music* of our daily lives. Do you "speak to yourself in psalms, hymns and spiritual songs" daily, or only in "designated assemblies"? What does this passage say about a Christian's preference for secular (non-Christian) radio – music and talk? Do we recoil at the thought of God telling us what kind of music and thoughts we should listen to "outside of church"? We'll talk more about these verses in our daily lives later.

Think also for a moment about singing to shut-ins or at nursing homes. To hear them tell it, those who listen to us receive a rich blessing. Exclusion thinks the Bible says that we must all sing, but then Exclusion replaces "God's" command with its own command that everyone merely have the *opportunity* to sing. It doesn't chastise folks at nursing homes for not trying to sing, though many who could sing choose to listen and not sing. It's the loophole. Our shut-ins, however, know the blessing of hearing others sing. It's the same blessing we have in listening to Christian singing groups on tape or after the closing prayer. It is a blessing we could have inside of our assemblies just as we do outside of them.

When a person begins to misunderstand a passage, one misunderstanding leads to another. Once you put on the *a cappella*-colored glasses, it becomes easier through those lenses to see anything that makes the *a cappella* arguments fit. God didn't create this loophole, but Exclusion demands it.

***Were you surprised?*** You knew that we approached the singing of God's praise differently inside versus outside of our assemblies. Were you surprised to see scholars establish this difference by applying New Testament singing verses *only* to "the public worship of the church"? Our young people cannot get past this chapter. They find Exclusion to be so inconsistent on this argument that they look no further.

***Who changed praise?*** We've looked at New Testament passages on how we live. Do the singing verses alone only apply to assemblies, to the exclusion of our daily (or "private") lives? Is the loophole a "necessary inference" for your singing doctrine? Do *you* take these singing verses out of their daily life contexts so that your other arguments can make sense? Are you careful to sing God's praise at times without calling it worship? Are *you* changing praise?

***Are you missing more than music?*** Drop the loophole. Be consistent. Be blessed by these passages as God intended them to be understood – in our everyday lives. Be guided by His passages on singing when you rise in the morning and when you go to bed at night. Surround yourself with God's word. Speak it and sing it to yourself and to others throughout the day. If God demands *a cappella*, all-together singing, then obey Him all the time without twisting the singing passages from their contexts. We must stop looking for ways to sing "How Great Thou Art" without calling it worship. We must stop playing word games with singing and worship.

Next, let's look at what the Bible calls "worship."

---

[1] Take for example the song "Butterfly Kisses," which launched the career of Bob Carlisle a decade ago. In it, the singer says, "I thank God for all the joy in my life, oh, but most of all for butterfly kisses after bedtime prayer...." [Bob Carlisle. "Butterfly Kisses." *Butterfly Kisses (Shades of Grace)*. CD. Benson. 1997.] Exclusion can listen to this accompanied soloist thank God in song on the radio or at a concert, but not in "public worship."

[2] Everett Ferguson, p. 17.

[3] Ferguson, p. 18.

[4] "The corporate nature of what is described in Ephesians 5:19 is made explicit by the 'one another' (cf. the same word in 4:32)." Ferguson, p. 17.

[5] See Ephesians 4:32 (as Ferguson suggests). Consider Colossians 3:13, I Thessalonians 5:13, Hebrews 3:13, and I Peter 4:8 and 10, etc.

[6] "Colossians adds that the 'word of the Lord' is to dwell 'among you,' 'in your midst.'" Ferguson, p.17

[7] "Moreover, Ephesians is making a contrast between pagan religious practices, where drunkenness and immorality were often associated with the cult, and Christian worship (verse 18)." Ferguson, p. 17.

[8] James McKinnon, *Music in Early Christian Literature* (Cambridge: Cambridge University Press, 1987), p.3.

[9] "Both Colossians and Ephesians are describing a setting where the word of the Lord is dispensed and song to God is engaged in." Ferguson, p.17.

[10] Ferguson, p.17.

[11] Ferguson, p. 22.

[12] How would you teach a song to people who can't read? It demands that others listen to praise as it is sung.

# The "Just Don't Call It Worship" Loophole
# Part 2: The Kind of Worshipers the Father seeks

What comes to mind when you think of "worship?" Do you mostly think of a Sunday assembly? *"Bible class is at 10, and worship is at 11."* Have you noticed that the New Testament never uses "worship" as a synonym for our "assembly?"

Read that last sentence again.

No New Testament word for worship has our assemblies as its primary focus. The *phrase* "worship assembly" doesn't appear in scripture. (And "worship leader" is an Old Testament concept.) For a people who pride ourselves with "calling Bible things by Bible names," we seem to have a certain ignorance of (or disregard for?) how the New Testament uses the word "worship." Our *a cappella*-colored glasses demand the "just don't call it worship" loophole when we look at verses on singing. Those same glasses also betray our misunderstanding of what the Bible calls "worship." They cloud our vision of the depths of God's heart for worship.

In this chapter, we will see that "worship" is hardly just another word for the public assembly of the Church. The focus of worship in the New Testament is our daily lives. Our assemblies are necessary, but the Bible never says that public assemblies offer a higher quality of worship. We will see that *any* time God's praise is sung, it is to be worship. Let's take a look at what the New Testament means when it says "worship."

## Why Does Greek Have Several Different Words for "Worship"?

The Chinese language has several different words for "uncle." They have one word for my father's older brother and a *different* word for his younger brother. Yet another two words are used for my *mother's* older and younger brothers, and another complete set of words are used for the *husbands* of my father's and my mother's older and younger sisters. They have different words for uncle because their culture places different demands on the respective relationships. All of their words may be translated "uncle," but that doesn't force the Chinese words to have the same meaning. In their culture, it matters which word for uncle one uses.

In the same way, several different Greek words are translated "worship" in English. Their meanings are not altered by my *one* English word. Rather, each of them has its own colorful meaning for us to discover. Those distinct differences are demonstrated in the ways that they are used in their contexts. Maybe you haven't seen the differences. As we look at different Greek words for worship and how they are used, we will also see that none of these words for "worship" is synonymous with "assembly."

## 1. Falling Down Worship - *prŏskunĕō*

The Greek word most commonly translated worship is *prŏskunĕō*. It occurs 54 times in the New Testament. Thayer defines it in the New Testament this way: "by kneeling or prostration to do homage (to one) or make obeisance, whether in order to express respect or to make supplication."[1] In deriving it, he mentions the Persian custom "to fall upon the knees and touch the ground with the forehead as an expression of profound reverence".[2] When you see **prŏskuněō**, think **pros**trate. It is an action, **never a noun**. In the King James Version, *prŏskuněō* is always translated "worship."

In this section, we will be talking about this act of worship that means to kneel or fall down. We will see that people dropped down to acknowledge their awe or to beg for grace. We will also see that this kind of worship is in no way bound primarily to assemblies.

Some of you may be surprised to learn that the New Testament's most common Greek word for worship means to fall because of respect and honor. To help you, I have quoted the following sample passages, all taken from the New International Version. I have **placed in bold** the English words translated from **prŏskuněō**. I have also *italicized* any *acts associated with this kind of worship*. As you read, notice when people *prŏskuněō*-worship, and notice the kinds of acts that are described by this verb.

Matt.2:11 On coming to the house, they saw the child with his mother Mary, and they *bowed down* and **worshiped** him. Then they opened their treasures and presented him with gifts of gold and of incense and of myrrh.

Matt.4:9 All this I will give you," he said, "if you will *bow down* and **worship** me."

Matt.8:2 A man with leprosy came and **knelt before** him and *said, "Lord, if you are willing*, you can make me clean."

Matt.9:18 While he was saying this, a ruler came and **knelt before** him and *said, "My daughter has just died. But come and put your hand on her, and she will live."*

Matt.14:33 Then those who were in the boat **worshiped** him, *saying, "Truly you are the Son of God."*

Matt.15:25 The woman came and **knelt before** him. *"Lord, help me!" she said.*

Matt.18:26 The servant *fell* **on his knees before** him. *'Be patient with me,' he begged,* 'and I will pay back everything.'

Matt.20:20 Then the mother of Zebedee's sons came to Jesus with her sons and, **kneeling down**, *asked a favor* of him.

Matt.28:9 Suddenly Jesus met them. "Greetings," he said. They came to him, *clasped his feet* and **worshiped** him.

Matt.28:17 When they saw him, they **worshiped** him; but some doubted.

Mark5:6-7 When he saw Jesus from a distance, he ran and **fell on his knees in front of** him. He *shouted* at the top of his voice, "What do you want with me, *Jesus, Son of the Most High God*? Swear to God that you won't torture me!"

Luke 4:7-8 So if you **worship** me, it will all be yours." Jesus answered, "It is written: '**Worship** the Lord your God and serve him only.'"

John 4:20 - 24 Our fathers **worshiped** on this mountain, but you Jews claim that the place where we must **worship** is in Jerusalem."

Jesus declared, "Believe me, woman, a time is coming when you will **worship** the Father neither on this mountain nor in Jerusalem. You Samaritans *worship* what you do not know; we **worship** what we do know, for salvation is from the Jews. Yet a time is coming and has now come when the true **worshipers** will **worship** the Father in spirit and truth, for they are the kind of **worshipers** the Father seeks. God is spirit, and his **worshipers** must **worship** in spirit and in truth."

John 9:38 Then the man *said, "Lord, I believe,"* and he **worshiped** him.

John 12:20 Now there were some Greeks among those who went up to **worship** at the Feast.

Acts 10:25 As Peter entered the house, Cornelius met him and *fell at his feet* in **reverence**.

Acts24:11 You can easily verify that no more than twelve days ago I went up to Jerusalem to **worship**.

1Cor.14:25 and the secrets of his heart will be laid bare. So he will *fall down* and **worship** God, *exclaiming, "God is really among you!"*

Rev.4:10-11 the twenty-four elders *fall down before* him who sits on the throne, and **worship** him who lives for ever

> and ever. They *lay their crowns before the throne and say: "You are worthy,* our Lord and God, to receive glory and honor and power, for you created all things, and by your will they were created and have their being."

Reading those passages alone may have led you to fall on your knees or put your face to the ground. Thayer (cited earlier) begins his definition of *pròskunĕō* with "*by kneeling or prostration to do homage* (to one) or *make obeisance.*" Sure enough, that is what we have seen. These are the acts of *pròskunĕō*-worship that we saw:

1) Kneeling
2) Falling down (sometimes on your face)
3) Giving praise or honor
4) Requesting something that only the one who is worshipped can provide

Interestingly, people literally dropped to the ground. None of them ever worried about what anyone besides God might think. It was completely irrelevant to them whether others might say …

> "That blind man just wants our attention."
> "Look at Jairus! He's just doing that to show off."
> "Can't that unclean leaper do his groveling in private?"
> "That behavior is embarrassing! What if a non-believer sees them and thinks we *all* do that? People won't want to follow God if they think we look ridiculous when we worship."

People *prostrated themselves in homage* because they were convicted. Concern over what *anybody* else thought never entered their minds.

The second part of Thayer's definition noted that the falling or kneeling was "*to express respect or to make supplication.*" We saw that, too.

We see people who *prostrated themselves in homage* because they recognized that their dire need was completely beyond their control – the leper, the mother, the father. Our personal tragedies, desperations, failures, and fears bring us to our knees. We acknowledge him who alone is able, and our posture bears witness before him that we are not.

Completely humbled, we call on the God of grace and mercy to hear us from on high.

And when God answers, we prostrate ourselves again. For we also see people who *prostrated themselves in homage* because they witnessed what God alone can do – those in the boat, those at the tomb, the once-blind man. When our prayers are answered by the otherwise inexplicable, we know that we have experienced the very hand of God. We are overcome by gratitude and by his presence. We fall to the ground and give honor to the God who is nothing if not faithful, loving, and holy. This is the kind of experience – the kind of worship – we live for ... and the kind we will also experience in heaven.

When Satan asked Jesus to worship him, he wasn't requesting a song, a gift, or a sermon from Jesus. He wanted everything. He wanted Jesus prostrate before him in reverence. No scene more devastating has ever been imagined.

Jesus and the woman at the well discussed the kind of worshipers *(pröskuněō)* the father seeks (John 4:20-24). Jesus said that under his reign, worship would no longer be seen as something that only happened in a certain place. Worship wouldn't be bound to certain rituals, ceremonies, and assemblies. God was looking for people who would bow the knee to him "in spirit and in truth." This worship is offered at any time.

It is odd that the most common word for worship in the New Testament is so uncommon today. **The closest we seem to come to this kind of worship is merely to *sing about* it, not actually to *do* it.** We sing, "Come let us worship and bow down. Let us kneel before the Lord our God, our maker" (Psalm 95:6), but we are hesitant to actually come bowing down or kneeling. Have you ever fallen to your knees with your face to the ground? In or out of an assembly, do you worship God this way, the way of the most common New Testament word for worship?

What about other acts we normally call "worship"? Did you notice what was missing from *pröskuněō's* definition and its passages? You didn't see preaching, taking the Lord's Supper, giving, or singing. It's not as though these assembly acts were not worship; they are. Examples of these acts are found with a *different* Greek word for worship (and service to God), but not with *pröskuněō*. Let's look at the word for our worship in song.

## 2. Every-Waking-Minute Worship - *latreia/latreuō*

The second most common Greek word that is often translated "worship" is *latreia* (the noun) or *latreuō* (the verb). *Latreia* (the **noun**) occurs 5 times in the New Testament. In the King James Version (KJV), it is always translated "service." The KJV translates *latreuō* (the **verb**) "serve" 16 times and "worship" 5 times. Modern English translations are more prone to translate both words as "worship."

Let's get a feel for *latreia/latreuō* in the New Testament. In the following passages from the New International Version (NIV), I have **placed in bold** words translated from *latreia/latreuō*, and I have *italicized examples of this service/worship.*

### λατρεια latreia (noun): service, worship

John 16:2 They will put you out of the synagogue; in fact, a time is coming when anyone who *kills you* will think he is *offering* a **service** to God.

Romans 9:4 the people of Israel. Theirs is the adoption as sons; theirs the divine glory, the covenants, the receiving of the law, the **temple worship** and the promises.

Romans 12:1 Therefore, I urge you, brothers, in view of God's mercy, to *offer your bodies as living sacrifices*, holy and pleasing to God--this is your spiritual act of **worship**.

Heb.9:1 Now the first covenant had regulations for **worship** and also an earthly sanctuary.

Heb.9:6 When everything had been arranged like this, the priests entered regularly into the outer room to carry on their **ministry**.

### λατρευω latreuō (verb): to serve, to worship

Matt. 4:10 Jesus said to him "Away from me, Satan! For it is written: 'Worship [*prŏskunĕŏ*] the Lord your God, and **serve** him only.'"

Luke 2:37 and then was a widow until she was eighty-four. She never left the temple but **worshiped** night and day, *fasting and praying.*

Acts 26:7 This is the promise our twelve tribes are hoping to see fulfilled as they earnestly **serve** God day and night. O king, it is because of this hope that the Jews are accusing me.

Acts 27:23 Last night an angel of the God whose I am and whom I **serve** stood beside me.

Romans 1:9 God, whom I **serve** with my whole heart *in preaching the gospel* of his Son, is my witness how constantly I remember you

Phil.3:3 For it is we who are the circumcision, we who **worship** *by the Spirit of God*, who glory in Christ Jesus, and who put no confidence in the flesh—

2 Tim. 1:3 I thank God, whom I **serve**, as my forefathers did, *with a clear conscience*, as night and day I constantly remember you in my prayers.

Heb.8:5 They **serve** at a sanctuary that is a copy and shadow of what is in heaven. This is why Moses was warned when he was about to build the tabernacle: "See to it that you make everything according to the pattern shown you on the mountain."

Heb.9:9 This is an illustration for the present time, indicating that the *gifts and sacrifices being offered* were not able to clear the conscience of the **worshiper**.

Heb.9:14 How much more, then, will the blood of Christ, who through the eternal Spirit offered himself unblemished to God, cleanse our consciences from acts that lead to death, so that we may **serve** the living God!

Heb.10:2 If it could, would they not have stopped being offered? For the **worshipers** would have been cleansed once for all, and would no longer have felt guilty for their sins.

Heb.12:28 Therefore, since we are receiving a kingdom that cannot be shaken, let us be thankful, and so **worship** God *acceptably with reverence and awe,*

> Re.22:3 No longer will there be any curse. The throne of God and of the Lamb will be in the city, and his servants [slaves] will **serve** him.

So, what did you learn about our assemblies? Exclusion has identified "five acts of worship" – preaching, singing, praying, giving, and taking the Lord's Supper. Are they worship? Yes, they are; they're *latreia/latreuō*. They are service-worship. But are they the *only* five acts of worship?

They are not. Fasting, too, is part of our service-worship to God (Luke 2:37). And what about offering our bodies as living sacrifices? What about all of our lives? Is that worship? Yes, it is (Romans 12:1). That is *latreia/latreuō*, too. All of our lives are dedicated to our service-worship to God. Again we see that *worship* and *assembly* are not synonymous in the New Testament.

In the settings that look back to the Old Covenant, you may have noticed that these Greek words typically refer to what the priests did in the temple. But you didn't find that emphasis in the New Testament settings. A dramatic shift is seen in the usage. The Romans destroyed the temple. Today, we understand that our songs of praise are just as much worship outside of an assembly as they are in one, because *all* of our lives must be worship. Offering God a gift, a prayer, a sermon, a song, a fast, a sacrifice – even a "24-7" living sacrifice – all of that is our service-worship to God. It's the same Greek word. It is all our service, our worship to Him, *all* the time.

## 3. Other Words for Worship

Other Greek words that are occasionally translated "worship" occur less often. If any were tied to assembled worship in the past, you will find that none of them are limited to or even primarily associated with an assembly after the death of Jesus.

*Sĕbōmai* means "to revere, to worship".[3] It occurs 10 times in the New Testament, almost always in the book of Acts. It is used of the "vain worship" practiced by the Pharisees[4] and of the worship of the idol

Artemis.[5] In Acts, it typically refers to the Gentile converts to Judaism, like Lydia when Paul found her (16:14).[6] Interestingly, it is not used to describe the worship of believers *after* their conversion to Jesus. Indeed, the Jews rightly complained that Christians don't "worship" (*sĕbŏmai*) the same any more (18:13).

The verb *lĕitŏurgia* (6 occurrences) means to minister or to serve. Its related noun, *lĕitŏurgĕŏ* (from which we get the English "liturgy") occurs 3 times and means ministry or service. In settings of the Old Testament, they refer to service of the priests (Luke 1:23, Hebrews 8:6; 9:21; 10:11). In settings of the New Testament, they are most often seen in the expressions of faithful living (Romans 15:27; 2 Cor. 9:12; Philippians 2:17, 30). In Acts 13:2, the noun is tied to a fast.

*Ĕusĕbĕŏ* (the verb, 2 occurrences)[7] and *ĕusĕbĕia* (the noun, 3 occurrences)[8] mean "to act reverently" and "godliness," respectively.[9] Ervin Bishop notes how under Jesus the meanings shifted from the performance of rituals to lifestyle.

> *The word* eusebeia *is rare in the New Testament and for most readers it would seem to be unrelated to the idea of worship, but it is of interest because of the way its usage contrasts with that in Greek literature. The popular Greek view was that religious piety consisted of honoring the gods, especially in worship paid to the gods in cultic acts. Paul's use of the verb in reference to the "worship" of the Athenians* [to the unknown god] *in Acts 17:23 was fitting. When used in reference to the Christian faith, however,* eusebeia *does not "consist in cultic acts as in the Greek world, not even in acts of congregational worship" (W. Foerster, TDNT, VII, p.183), but refers to a Christian's manner of life.*[10]

*Thrēskĕia* occurs only four times and means "religious worship, esp. external, that which consists in ceremonies."[11] Paul uses the word in this sense in describing his former way of life as a Pharisee (Acts 26:5) and of the false worship of angels (Col. 2:18). In contrast, Christian worship consists of daily life activity like controlling our tongues (James 1:26) and caring for "widows and orphans in their distress" (James 1:27).

# Summary

What have we learned from our study of the New Testament words for worship? In the New Testament, no word for Christian worship is bound to our "designated assemblies." There is no exception. Christianity is not compartmentalized into "worship" when we come together versus "non-worship" after the closing prayer. There is no exemption from worship in our "private" lives. We are called to worship in the daylight and in the dark, in our work and in our play, in our homes and in our cars, in weddings and in funerals, and in VBS.

In John 4, the Samaritan woman's question is about *where* we worship. She wondered on which mountain believers should worship. Jesus said a time was coming when the mountain wouldn't matter. Indeed, today God's temple is not on a mountain. God's temple is each of his believers. Under the Old Testament, believers would come and go from that temple. Under the New Testament, believers never leave the temple. Or better said, God never leaves the temple that we are, in or out of an assembly.

What is the point of this chapter? Exclusion says that its rules against solos and instruments are only binding on our public worship assemblies. It says that we can attend funerals where solos and instruments are heard, because "it's not worship." It says that our children can clap and dance in VBS, because "it's not worship." It says we can sing Christmas songs with the radio, because "it's not worship." It says that we can sing to shut-ins, because "it's not worship." It says that we can have a piano in our wedding (if we go somewhere else), because "it's not worship." To the contrary, all of our praise is worship! **A closing prayer may dismiss us from an assembly, but *nothing* dismisses us from worship.**

First, Exclusion said that the New Testament verses on singing only apply to assemblies, despite the daily-life context of their surrounding verses. (We studied that in the previous chapter.) Now, Exclusion tells us that worship itself only applies to our public assemblies. It is as though we can sing God's praise at any other time without calling it worship! Exclusion is led to these conclusions by its premise that the New Testament must have dictated the chant of the early church. It exempts praise outside of its assemblies by charging that such songs are not worship. It is blind not only to its premise but also to the impact of that premise in re-defining worship.

# Can Christians Sing in an Assembly?

In the following chapters, we will begin to look at Bible words for singing. As we look at these words, remember that they are used of our praise ALL THE TIME, not just in our "worship assemblies." In fact, every New Testament reference to singing is outside of the context of a designated Christian assembly, except one: 1 Corinthians 14:15, 26. If instruments, choruses, and solos are excluded from songs of praise, then they are ALWAYS excluded. Whatever the rules are, there are no exemptions – neither for Vacation Bible Schools nor Christmas music nor "Sunday night new songs" nor weddings nor funerals nor youth gatherings nor concerts nor Christian radio nor singing and playing a new song to learn how it goes at home – nor for "worship assemblies." Christians sing praise the same in an assembly and out of it; the same rules apply. Can we Christians sing in our assemblies? Yes, only and fully in the same ways we can sing outside of them.

***Were you surprised?*** For years I had heard arguments that the Bible used one word for worship in our assemblies and a *different* word for worship at other times. Were you surprised that the word for worship in songs and prayers (at any time) is the same word for worship as a living sacrifice? All of our songs of praise are equally worship, inside and outside of an assembly.

***Who changed praise?*** Jesus said that our worship is no longer tied to a physical setting. Who changed that? Are we "the kind of worshiper our father seeks," or have we "dismissed worship" outside of Christian assemblies? Who limited Christian worship to five acts – singing praise, praying, preaching, giving, and sharing the Lord's Supper – to the exclusion of other Biblical acts of worship, like fasting or offering yourself as a living sacrifice? Who said that those five acts are only worship if they're in an assembly, as though they might be offered outside of an assembly without worshiping? Do we ever fall on our knees in worship to God, or do we just sing about it? Contrary to the Bible, do we use "worship" as a synonym for Christian assemblies?

***Are you missing more than music?*** We must fight the temptation to judge the posture of other worshippers in our assemblies. A reward awaits us if we do not judge those who fall to their knees or lift their hands. We may see how God interacts with those who come to him in ways that are uncomfortable to us.

Remember that Jesus' first disciples at times disapproved of the way others approached him and even tried to stop them. An example is the blind man at Jericho. As Jesus was passing him by, Bartimaeus cried out for mercy. Sadly, "those who led the way rebuked him" (Luke 18:39). Once again (compare 18:16), Jesus overruled them. When Jesus was done, everyone was praising God (18:43). Think what they would have missed!

I have watched a newly divorced woman lift holy hands in the pew beside me and yet sing, "For all that you've done I will thank you." I have turned around to watch my friend Mark dance in worship in the back, and I think I see David. I wouldn't miss that kind of praise.

Finally, we must quit identifying *worship* as an assembly. We must worship God with all of our lives. Let our songs of praise be acceptable to him just the same whether we're learning a song for the first time or singing by memory, whether we prefer the song or not, whether we're in a Sunday assembly or at a funeral or alone in our cars, whether we're teaching a song or learning one, let it all – always – be *worship* to God.

---

[1] Joseph Henry Thayer, *A Greek-English Lexicon of the New Testament* (Grand Rapids, MI: Baker Book House, 1977), entry 4352, p. 548.

[2] Thayer, p. 548.

[3] Thayer, 572.

[4] Matt. 15:9; Mark 7:7.

[5] Acts 19:27.

[6] Paul sought out the Jews first whenever he entered a town (Acts 17:2). He found these Gentile converts to Judaism at Pisidion Antioch (Acts13:43,50), Philippi (16:14), Thessalonica (17:4), Athens (17:17), and Corinth (18:7).

[7] Acts 17:23 and I Tim 5:4.

[8] I Tim 2:2; 3:16; 4:7, 8; 6:3,5,6,11; 2 Tim 3:5; 2 Peter 1:3,6,7; and 3:11.

[9] Thayer, p. 262.

[10] Ervin Bishop, "The Christian Assembly (2)," *Firm Foundation*, 90, No. 10 (March 13, 1973).

[11] Thayer, p. 292.

Exclusion's Third
Disputable Matter:

"The New Testament is Silent
on Singing Praise with Any
Accompaniment"

# Looking for Evidence

Those who allow instrumental accompaniment in praise see themselves as a part of a rich tradition of God's people dating back thousands of years, preceding even the Old Covenant. Despite this history, however, Exclusion argues that God currently does not approve of instruments in praise. (To be consistent, many also forbid clapping.) In the chapters of this section, we're going to be evaluating the evidence to see whether the New Testament ended accompaniment in songs of praise when Jesus died.

First, think of the kind of evidence that you might suppose would prove that God had indeed changed praise. What kind of Biblical evidence would you expect to find? Let's begin by compiling a list of what should be the obvious signs that God changed praise. Our list would include verses like these.

- Any passages that *condemn* the use of the musical instruments or clapping in Christian praise,

- Any verses that *prophesy* the end of instruments or clapping in songs of praise,

- Any scriptures that *give reasons for* this change in songs of praise ushered in by Jesus' death, and

- Any verses that explicitly *command* spoken words <u>only</u> in our songs today.

After all of our study, these are the passages we would have:

**[This paragraph intentionally left blank.]**

It's not what you would expect, is it? Indeed, if Exclusion were convinced that the first century church used instruments in praise, then it would find no contradiction with any passage of scripture in the Old or New Testaments.

Read that last sentence again.

How, then, can Exclusion forbid instruments? It's not as though God were never pleased with accompaniment in songs of praise; he certainly was. God *asked* for musical instruments. Exclusion merely alleges that God hasn't asked for them *lately*. Exclusion asks to be shown that God *still* appreciates accompaniment in songs of praise.

We can be certain that many Old Testament commands were nailed to the cross, because God said so. We can also be certain that many Old Testament commands (like the greatest ones) remain, because God also said so. Although God never called for an end to instrumental accompaniment in praise, Exclusion wants to be sure that accompaniment remains. That is the evidence we will be looking for.

These next few chapters will not only refute arguments that God now *opposes* instruments or clapping in praise, but they will also present evidence that God still *accepts* accompaniment in praise.

- The next chapter will look at the **New Testament commands** for our singing to see if they can be interpreted in a way that allows <u>only</u> *a cappella* songs of praise.

- The chapter after that will consider **Old Testament prophecy.** We need to look at prophecy that Jesus fulfilled regarding praise in our day.

- Still looking at prophecy, a third chapter will examine what Exclusion suggests could be **God's *motivation*** for ending accompaniment when Jesus died.

Remember, whatever we find will be binding on our praise at any time, not just during Sunday morning assemblies.

After this section on accompaniment, a different section will look at solos and choruses. Let's look now at the evidence for accompaniment in praise.

# *A Cappella* isn't in the Bible

Exclusion believes that *a cappella* singing is important to God, important enough for us to separate ourselves from other Christians who allow accompaniment. Exclusion cannot teach us to sing praise today without using words like "*a cappella*" or "without instruments." Oddly, those phrases are not found in the Bible.

Now don't misunderstand. Those who love God certainly praise him without accompaniment in both the Old and New Testaments, just as they are seen praising him *with* accompaniment in both.[1] But if we are to praise God "<u>only</u> *a cappella*" for now, we must be curious about why these central phrases never occur in scripture. We must wonder how English translations of the inspired word can teach us to sing God's praise without ever using the words that seem indispensable to *our* teaching of "New Testament praise" today.

But we haven't yet gone far enough. It's not just that *our* vocabulary is missing, but rather that vocabulary we consider misleading *is* there. The terminology of the English New Testament seems to contradict the "*a cappella* only" appraisal. The New Testament bids us to "sing psalms," which are full of instruments. It calls us to "sing and make music," a phrase reserved for accompanied singing elsewhere in the Bible (e.g.: Psalms 57:7-8; 108:1-2). It has Christian martyrs "*singing*" with "harps of God" in visions of Heaven. Honestly, our English New Testaments seem a bit unfriendly to the "*a cappella* <u>only</u>" interpretation.

But we must go further still. Scholars who translate the Bible say that they *intended* to include accompaniment as acceptable in Christian praise. Tom Burgess devotes an entire chapter of his *Documents on Instrumental Music* to the testimony of translators who responded to his request for clarification. These scholars assure us that their wording was purposely chosen to embrace the option of instruments in Christian praise.[2]

Nevertheless, Exclusion argues that God opposes accompaniment in the public worship of the church.

Now, in fairness, there are indeed times when our English translations come up short. Exclusion argues that this is one of those times. It contends that a close look at the New Testament Greek words for singing will persuade honest people to praise God "only *a cappella*." It invites us to look at Greek lexicons. (A lexicon is a kind of dictionary that looks at how words were derived and how they were used in their day in order to show their meanings.) In this chapter, we wade into Greek lexicons because Exclusion asks us to.

## What are We Looking For?

Before we wade in, however, it is important to ask what we are looking for. Exclusion concludes that we should sing God's praise only *a cappella* because of the meanings of the New Testament words that we are about to look at. It is interesting, however, that the early church chanted without ever making that argument. As we will see, none of these New Testament words meant to praise God *a cappella* only. If they had, then the early church might have cited that as a reason for their chant. In other words, as we consider these definitions, remember that we are looking at *Exclusion's* arguments, not arguments from the earliest church. In the chapter on history, we asked about *their* reasons for chanting. In this chapter, Exclusion has asked us to look at its own reasons. The English New Testament does not have our language, and the early Church did not make our arguments for singing exclusively *a cappella*. Exclusion is introducing a modern argument for *a cappella* that the early church never made.

Now here is a word of caution. Those who embrace accompaniment and those who oppose it look at the same lexicons and each conclude that their own position is justified. One group sees "*a cappella* also;" the other sees "*a cappella* only." We will continue to see evidence that one's belief about why the early church chanted explains what one finds in the scriptures. If you are not careful, what you already think about instruments will color what you find.

## 'Sing' Means 'Sing'

If you are familiar with the debate, you have heard the argument that "'Sing' means 'sing'." The argument alleges that if New Testament Greek words are translated with the English word "sing," then we can only say that they mean "sing," and nothing more. The implication is that they mean "sing *a cappella*." Since even the English word "sing" is not restricted to the meaning, "sing *a cappella*," we must ask where the argument comes from. Again, whenever an argument is puzzling, it helps to consider the influence of Exclusion's premise, that the early church chanted by command of God.

If one holds Exclusion's premise, then he naturally looks at scripture from that perspective. He presumes that the scriptures teach "*a cappella*" unless he can be persuaded otherwise. It is a sort of "prove me wrong" approach. He mentally views commands to sing as though they said "sing *a cappella*," because that interpretation alone fits his premise. He argues that we cannot "add" accompaniment to the passages. He doesn't see that he has added "*a cappella*." We might as easily presume that the scriptures say "sing with or without instruments," and then ask others to prove that singing had to be *a cappella*. Again, the scriptures don't say "*a cappella*."

This "prove me wrong" approach to Bible study (based on one's view of history, not scripture) has big implications as we begin our study of Greek words for "sing." It reminds us to guard against two misunderstandings about how words are translated.

First, "'sing' means 'sing'" mistakenly suggests that the meanings of Biblical Greek words may be reduced to the meanings of the English words that translate them. "'Greek-word' means 'sing'" incorrectly implies that these Greek words can have no meaning beyond "sing."

If you have studied a foreign language, you will remember how often your teacher would say, "We don't have a word for this." Although you would translate the foreign word into English, you would recognize that the foreign word had a broader meaning. In this same way, we will see that at least one of these Greek words for our praise in song has definitions that are *never* used to define "sing." These Greek words don't merely mean English "sing."

Second, "'sing' means 'sing (*a cappella*)'" incorrectly leads Exclusion to dispute any lexicon that argues for meanings beyond "*a cappella*." We will see that Exclusion argues for the elimination of meanings of words as they were used in the first century, even in the Bible. *Exclusion does not merely prefer secondary meanings, but rather declares accepted meanings to be non-meanings.* It wants us to conclude that all of the Greek words for sing shared one pro-*a cappella* meaning.

In this chapter, Exclusion asks us to put the translators on trial. We will read the various definitions and see how these words were used in their contexts. Then we must ask what you would have done if you had been a translator. Would you have been the first translator to use the words that Exclusion finds essential to New Testament teaching on singing? Would you have used phrases like "*a cappella* only" or "without instruments"?

## Singing in Greek

There are basically six Greek words for singing in the New Testament – three nouns and three related verbs. The three nouns (for "song") are *psalmos*, from which English derives "psalm"; *humnos*, for hymn; and *ōdē*, for ode. The associated verb forms (for "sing") of these Greek nouns are *psallō*, *humneō*, and *ádō*, respectively. We might think of them as meaning psalming, hymning, and ode-ing. The Bible identifies all six words with Christian praise.

In fact, Paul uses five of the six words (all but hymning) when he addresses disciples in Ephesians 5:19. Identifying them in that passage, we read:

"...Speaking to yourselves in **psalms** [*psalmos*] and **hymns** [*humnos*] and spiritual **songs** [*ōdē*]. **Singing** [*ádō*] and **making melody** [*psallō*] in your heart to the Lord."

Are there any implications for Paul's use of all of these Greek words? Our preachers often argue that when Paul wrote this letter, he intended his Christian readers to understand that *all* of these Greek singing words in this context implied *expressly a cappella* singing in the minds of his first century recipients. They contend that Paul would have been *surprised* if the Ephesians had somehow misunderstood him and permitted instruments.

So, what do the Greek "singing" words mean? Let's look at their meanings and consider their meanings in their contexts.

## *Ōdē* and *Ádō*
### ("What is Greek for 'Singing' ... in Heaven?")

*Ōdē* and *ádō* always occur together in the New Testament. They mean song[3] and sing,[4] respectively. Besides Ephesians 5:19 and Colossians 3:16, they only occur in the Revelation of John, in 5:9, 14:3, and 15:3. All three instances in John's Revelation occur with harps (or the sound of harps) specified in the preceding verse. Let's take a look.

In Revelation 14, John hears what sounds like "harpists playing their harps" (14:2). The music is as loud as thunder, like the "roar of rushing waters." And with this music, he hears the 144,000 singing [*ádō*] a new song [*ōdē*] (verse 3). John doesn't seem surprised to hear harps. He uses these same words for singing songs of praise that Paul uses; yet John doesn't think that they demand *a cappella* in the context of worship. In Revelation 5: 8, 9, John sees the creatures of Heaven also singing a new song, and each of them has his own harp. Similarly, in Revelation 15:2, 3, those who have been victorious over the beast hold "harps given them by God" and sing the song of Moses and the Lamb. [This reminds us of how those in the Old Testament praised God with "the Lord's instruments" (2 Chronicles 7:6 and 30:21).]

John's use of *ōdē* and *ádō* is very hard to square with "*a cappella* only." Few would argue that God is handing out harps because he likes to see them but not hear them. In fact, John tells us that the harps are thunderously loud in chapter 14.

Exclusion typically dismisses these passages by saying that the use of accompaniment in Heaven would not authorize it on Earth. That much is true, but we are talking about the meanings of words. When the church at Ephesus received *Paul's* letter, Exclusion asks us to believe that they understood *ōdē* and *ádō* to have an **unmistakably** *a cappella* meaning. We are told that Paul would have been *surprised* if the Ephesians thought his language meant *anything* but *a cappella*. Yet when the same church receives *John's* Revelation (see Revelation 2:1), the only thing **unmistakable** about *ōdē* and *ádō* is the *presence* of instruments and accompaniment *in all three contexts*, not their absence.

Exclusion also discounts the weight of this argument by asserting that the instruments are symbolic.[5] But again, whether the instruments are symbolic or not, Exclusion must contend that Paul *banishes* instruments from worship in Ephesians and Colossians with these same first century Greek words that John uses consistently in three different chapters to *include* accompaniment in worship! In the context of worship in first century Greek, *ōdē* and *ádō* cannot mean to sing songs "*a cappella* only."

Exclusion assigns a meaning to these words when Paul uses them of praise that it cannot defend when John uses them of praise. It excuses the difference by saying that John was speaking of Heaven or speaking symbolically. Here again we see Exclusion accepting a contradiction in order to harmonize scriptures with its belief that the early church chanted by command of God. Exclusion believes that Paul *must* have meant something different from John, so it finds ways to dismiss John's usage.

It is noteworthy that John doesn't feel compelled to say that anyone was singing "and playing." In chapters 5 and 15, there is no second Greek verb for "playing harps." Rather, he describes accompanied singing with one Greek verb – *ádō*. In John's mind, *ádō* (the verb) encompasses *singing with accompaniment* all by itself in all three worship contexts. Moreover, these accompanied songs are simply called *ōdē* (the noun).

After decades of presumably retraining Jewish Christians[6] to sing exclusively *a cappella*, John uses *ōdē* and *ádō* alone to describe the singing of praise that is NOT *a cappella*. If *ōdē* and *ádō must* mean "*a cappella*" in worship contexts, then John doesn't know Greek … and neither does the Spirit of God who inspired him. If "sing means sing" – if *ōdē* and *ádō* have only one meaning in all contexts, as Exclusion implies – then it is *impossible* that the meaning could be "*a cappella* only." (What is it about harps that God likes? We will return to the question of what he likes in the next chapter.) It is easy to see why the early church never defended their chant by arguing that *ōdē* and *ádō* demand *a cappella* singing only.

Exclusion has difficulty explaining how *ōdē* and *ádō* are used. The difficulty in this next pair of Greek word is in how they are *defined*.

## *Psallō* (the Verb)

*Psallō*, our next Greek verb for sing, is never defined without mention of instruments. (Its related noun gives us our word for "psalm.") It was used in common, first century Greek for strumming on an instrument, though this was no longer its primary definition. You will see lexicons that tell you its primary meaning was to sing with instruments. You will see lexicons that say that its primary meaning was to sing with or without instruments. You will not find a lexicon that says that in first century it meant to sing *a cappella*.

It will perhaps surprise you to learn that Exclusion's scholars do not unanimously dispute this first century meaning of *psallō*. Indeed, Ferguson concedes the instrumental implications of the word *outside of* the New Testament. He writes, "Hellenistic Jews writing for Gentile audiences kept to the classical meaning of *psallō*."[7] Put more clearly, Greek-speaking Jews (like those in Acts 2 and 6) always used *psallō* in the instrumental sense when writing to Gentiles. Ferguson provides examples of two first century, Hellenistic Jews who were prolific writers – Josephus and Philo. Though not Christians, these contemporaries of Paul wrote in the same common (called "Koine") Greek as the New Testament.[8] Ferguson assures us that the historian Josephus *always* used *psallō* in an instrumental sense.[9] In contrast, the philosopher Philo never used the word at all. As a first century champion of *a cappella* (and "silent") singing, his influence was felt for centuries. In guessing why Philo never used *psallō*, Ferguson offers, "A plausible hypothesis would be that Philo is aware of the primarily instrumental connotation of the word to pagan readers."[10] Wow! As we look at the definition of *psallō* in the fist century Greek lexicons, you will see the same instrumental implications that Ferguson is talking about.

How can Exclusion's chief scholar acknowledge the first century, instrumental implications of *psallō*, you ask? It's like this. Ferguson speculates that *psallō* took on an *a cappella* meaning only in "Jewish religious language."[11] He argues that *psallō* was becoming something different – *a cappella* only – in "Jewish religious language" alone. We will address this argument after you have watched for it in the lexicons. Let's see how the scholars define *psallō* in common, first century Greek.

Here are the first century definitions of *psallō* from numerous Greek lexicons in order by publication date. I have numbered them so that we can refer back to them next.

> **1. Thayer, 1901.** *to sing to the music of the harp;* in the N.T. [New Testament] *to sing a hymn, to celebrate the praises of God.*[12]

Let's pause here. We've barely begun, but this is a good time to stop and take a closer look at this first definition. Before we read any others, let's consider how the beliefs that we bring to our study may affect what we see when looking at the same evidence. What could lead two people to reach different conclusions about *a cappella* singing from this lexicon? Review Thayer's definition and continue on.

Exclusion believes that the early church chanted by command of God. In the past, when I looked at Thayer's definition through Exclusion's eyes, I saw some extra, *"italicized"* words that weren't really there. I thought that Thayer was saying that *psallō "used to mean"* sing to the music of the harp. But Thayer doesn't say "used to mean," does he? Exclusion's perspective trained me to think that Thayer was contrasting *psallō* in the past (when it *"used to"* include harps) with *psallō* "in the New Testament *times."* But Thayer doesn't make his contrast with "New Testament *times."* He merely notes that in first century common Greek, *psallō* was not a church word. It could be used of both sacred *and* secular accompanied singing. However, "in the New Testament" it is only used of sacred songs. The added, italicized words were seen only with an *a cappella* lens.

I was missing more than music. I parsed Thayer's definition as though his primary purpose were to answer my questions about instruments. By adding the italicized words, I actually missed his primary purpose. He was telling me that any time I saw *psallō* in the New Testament, I should understand that it was talking about praise. When James says, "Is any [among you] merry? let him sing psalms" (James 5:13; KJV), he doesn't mean to sing just any happy song, but rather a song of praise. That's what separates *psallō* in the New Testament from *psallō* outside of it. Following Thayer, modern versions translate *psallō* in James 5:13 with "sing praise," not just "sing psalms." James says our happiness should spill over into songs of Heaven, not songs of Earth – songs by *Third Day*, not *Green Day*.

I saw an italicized mirage. The illusion blinded me to what the scholars say is truly distinctive about *psallō* in the New Testament. I wanted to see, but I couldn't see. Unaffected by the mirage, the translators tell us to sing praise; not one says to sing *a cappella*. *A cappella* is itself an italicized word that Exclusion sees in the New Testament, a word that never appears on any page.

Allowing accompaniment, by the way, is consistent with how Thayer translates *psallō*'s related noun, *psalmos*. When Thayer discusses the three synonym nouns for Christian "songs" (the words for psalm, hymn, and song), he repeats Bishop Lightfoot. Specifically on Colossians 3:16, Thayer quotes Lightfoot, "...the leading idea of *psalm* is a musical accompaniment...."[13] Adding *a cappella* to Thayer's definition of *psallō* would also contradict Thayer's definition of *psalm* in the specific New Testament context of Colossians 3:16. One might argue that Thayer is wrong, but we must not change what he says by putting italicized words in his mouth.

Read Thayer's definition once more. Then, as you study what the following scholars have to say about *psallō* in their lexicons, be aware of how your perspective may color what you see. This awareness gives us hope that what we find will not be merely a reflection of what we already believe. It opens the door to resolving our disagreement and discovering more than our issue.

2. **Arndt and Gingrich, 1957.** in our lit., in accordance with OT usage, *sing (to the accompaniment of a harp), sing praise* with dative of the one for whom the praise is intended.... In [Eph. 5:19] a second dative is added ... *in your heart(s)*....[14]

3. **Liddell and Scott, 1968.** Later, *sing to a harp*, Lxx [Septuagint] Psalm 7:17, 9:11, al.; τη καρδια [in your heart] Eph 5:19; τω πνευματι [with my spirit] I Cor. 14:15.[15]

4. **Delling, 1972.** [Of the Septuagint translation of the Psalms:] often the obvious sense is "to play," especially when an instrument is mentioned ... Psalms 27:6; 57:7; 101:1; 105:2; 108:1, where singing and playing go together, *v.* also Psalms 18:49, 57:9 (cf. v. [see verse] 8), 108:3 (cf. v. 2). Elsewhere the idea of praise by song as well as stringed instrument is suggested, Psalms 9:11; 30:4; 66:4.... [Of some other contexts] one must take into account a shift in meaning in the LXX [Septuagint] in other passages in which the idea of playing is not evident.[16]

[Delling acknowledges that *psallō* and/or *psalmos* (the related noun) continue to be used for "playing an instrument" during and after the days of the Apostles, citing Plutarch, Lucian, and Josephus as examples. -DRC][17]

[Referring to Ephesians 5:19:] What is meant is "the engagement of the heart," not "silent song."[18] ... The literal sense of "by or with the playing of strings," still found in the LXX, is now employed figuratively.[19]

5. **Gingrich and Danker, 1979.** in our lit., in accordance with OT usage, *sing, sing praise* with dative of the one for whom the praise is intended.... In [Eph. 5:19] a second dative is added ... *in or with your heart(s)*; here it is found with *ádō* ... and the question arises whether a contrast between the two words is intended. The original meaning of *psallō* was 'pluck', 'play' (a stringed instrument); this persisted at least to the time of Lucian [circa 160 A.D.]. In the LXX [Septuagint],

psallō frequently means 'sing', whether to the accompaniment of a harp or (as usually) not.... Although the New Testament does not voice opposition to instrumental accompaniment, in view of Christian opposition to mystery cults, as well as Pharisaic aversion to musical instruments in worship... it is likely that some such sense as make melody is best here [Eph 5:19]. Those who favor 'play' (e.g. L-S-J; A. Souter, Pocket Lexicon, 1920; J. Moffatt, translation, 1913) may be relying too much on the earliest meaning of *psallō*.[20]

6. **Wingram, 1983.** *to play on a stringed instrument; to sing to music;* in N.T. *to sing praises.*[21]

7. **Louw and Nida, 1988.** To sing songs of praise, with the possible implication of instrumental accompaniment (in the New Testament often related to the singing of OT psalms).[22]

8. **NTGED, 1991.** It is widely agreed that the primary meaning in the New Testament is "to sing" with at least the possible nuance of "to sing with a musical instrument." Clearly no conclusions can be drawn solely from the lexical meaning of psallō as to whether instrumental accompaniment should be included with Christian worship in song.[23]

9. **Zodhiates, 1992.** to touch lightly, twang or snap. To play a stringed instrument or to sing a hymn. Musicians who play upon an instrument were said to pluck the strings.... The word came to signify making music in any fashion. Because stringed instruments were commonly used by both believers and heathen in singing praises to their respective gods, it meant to sing, sing praises or psalms to God whether with or without instruments.[24]

10. **Danker, 2000.** in our lit., in accordance with OT usage, **to sing songs of praise, with or without instrumental accompaniment,** *sing, sing praise....*[25]

What did we learn from the lexicons? Here is what we know about *psallō* in the days of the Apostles:

- The widely accepted primary meaning of *psallō* is to sing with or without instruments, though instrumental accompaniment may be implied.

- It is disputed whether *psallō* was used for "play" outright (as distinct from "sing with accompaniment") in the New Testament, though it was used for "play" in the common Greek of the day (and for generations afterward).

- Although *psallō* was not a religious word, it is only used of praise to God in the New Testament.

- The stated arguments against instrumental accompaniment in songs of praise are extra-Biblical, based neither on the word *psallō* itself nor on Biblical texts.

Maybe I caught you off guard with that last statement. Perhaps you rather thought that some of the scholars argue that *psallō* indeed meant to chant in the first century, just as it does today. Let's review three lexicons where preconceptions might slant what a person sees.

Delling (example 4) believes that *psallō* has a limited, *a cappella* meaning in the New Testament as distinct from the common Greek of the first century, but he doesn't explain why.

- He cites several authors from the Apostles' day who used *psallō* for playing instruments in common Greek. He does *not* deny the instrumental implications of the word in general.

- He says that in the Septuagint (the Greek translation of the Old Testament), *psallō* meant "play" in at least a couple of scenarios:

  o In Psalms 18:49; 57:9; and 108:3. (This is David's prophecy for our day, cited by Paul in Romans 15:9. We'll examine this prophecy in the next chapter.)

  o Virtually anywhere *psallō* occurs with its synonym *ádō* (Psalms 27:6; 57:7; 101:1; 105:2; 108:1). (This is the same pairing Paul uses of our singing in Ephesians 5:19.)

- He rules out "silent singing" in the New Testament. What is silent singing, you ask? Do you remember the first century Jewish philosopher and champion of *a cappella* singing who never used *psallō*? Ferguson explains that "Philo recognized that even the voice is inadequate to the praise of God.... [T]here occurs in a few passages the concept of 'silent singing' as the highest type of praise."[26] Delling calls us to follow Philo selectively, silencing strings but not vocal chords.

- He does not explain why he believes that the Biblical writers might use *psallō* in a more restricted sense than other writers of their day, whom he has cited.

NTGED (example 8) concedes that instrumental accompaniment may be implied "in the New Testament," but adds that we should look beyond the *definition* of *psallō* to determine its *usage* in the New Testament. It points us to Danker.

Thankfully, Danker (examples 5 and 10, above) tells us *why* he thinks *psallō* does not imply instruments in the New Testament. You should notice that the Lexicon of Walter Bauer has been translated into English three times. It was translated first by Arndt and Gingrich in 1957 (example 2), then by Gingrich and Danker in 1979 (example 5), and finally by Danker alone in 2000 (example 10).

- Example 2: Arndt and Gingrich say that *psallō* means to sing with or without accompaniment.

- Example 5: When Danker replaces Arndt, the entry for *psallō* changes. Gingrich's influence produces the reference to Lucian, who still used *psallō* for "play" a stringed instrument (as distinct from "sing with accompaniment") long after the days of the apostles. Danker's influence counters that *psallō* probably didn't mean "play" in Ephesians 5. Unlike Delling, Danker tells us why: (a) the first century Pharisees didn't like the instruments that God had commanded for them and (b) the early church didn't like idol-worshiping cults. (In the chapter on the chant, we looked at his arguments for limiting the meaning of *psallō* in the New Testament.)

- Example 10: What is most interesting is what Danker does when given the chance to edit the Bauer translation by himself. In 2000, the only revision Danker makes to the entry for *psallō* is to re-insert (in BOLD) the original thought of Arndt and Gingrich, that the primary first century meaning of *psallō* is to sing with or without instruments. Danker still argues that *psallō* may not mean "play" alone in the New Testament (though he concedes that it does outside of the New Testament). Curiously, Danker sings a different tune with a change he brings to the companion entry for *ádō*. There Danker inserts this translation of Eph 5:19: *"singing and playing (instrumentally) heartily to the Lord."*[27] In modifying both entries, Danker makes it clearer that the word *psallō* itself did not mean "sing *a cappella* only" when the New Testament was written.

Again, the stated arguments against instrumental accompaniment in songs of praise are extra-Biblical, based neither on the word *psallō* itself nor on Biblical texts.

Nevertheless, Exclusion typically argues that *psallō* had only one meaning in the first century, and that the one meaning was *a cappella*. While others find harmony among the lexicons, Exclusion draws a dividing line, marking lexicons that are the most unfavorable to it as unreliable and dogmatic. It is an awkward position to defend. In truth, every lexicon acknowledges instruments in its first century definition of *psallō*; there is *no* exception. The case for an *a cappella* **usage** of *psallō* in the New Testament comes from cultural considerations, not from any *a cappella* definition in the first century and not from any anti-instrument language in the Bible.

Put another way, no lexicon teaches what Exclusion commonly asserts, that *psallō* had completely changed its meaning in the first century. The closest that selected lexicons come is to say that the meaning in the New Testament might not demand accompaniment.

This is a good place to return to Ferguson's arguments. Remember he said that Greek-speaking Jews writing to Gentiles always used *psallō* in the instrumental sense. He said that this explained why (1) Josephus used *psallō* only with instruments, and (2) Philo avoided *psallō* when encouraging Greeks to praise only *a cappella*. The hypothesis struggles. Josephus' example might imply that Paul, writing to Greeks at Ephesus,[28] would also have used *psallō* in the instrumental sense, which Ferguson disputes. Philo's example says that he avoided *psallō* because he was addressing Greeks, yet Ferguson admits, "It is disputed whether Philo was writing primarily for Gentiles or for his own people."[29] We should also note if *psallō* had a different meaning in "Jewish religious language," then Philo would have been free to use it to promote his *a cappella* praise, but he never did. Ferguson proposes patterns which he cannot demonstrate.

There is yet another *psallō* defense offered by Exclusion that we did not find in the lexicons. Exclusion proposes that if *psallō* means "play" in Ephesians 5:19, then the instrument identified as being strummed in that verse is the heart. Scholars, however, tell us that the Greek syntax demands that both the singing and the playing engage the same heart. If we sing audibly with the heart, then we also play audibly with the heart. Engaging the heart silences neither.[30] For clarity, consider the result if we apply Exclusion's argument to Psalm 108:1, 2. To be consistent, we would say that David was plucking the strings of his soul in verse 1, and then run aground of the harp and lyre specified in verse 2. David sang and played musical instruments with all his soul. In the same way, singing and playing musical instruments with all our hearts satisfies Ephesians 5:19.

Note that Exclusion's arguments regarding *psallō* not only contradict the lexicons, but also each other. One argument says that *psallō* had changed meanings entirely and meant *a cappella* everywhere in the first century. Another argument acknowledges that *psallō* broadly implied instruments in the first century, yet proposes an exception for Greek-speaking Jewish Christians only when they wrote in religious contexts. A final argument concedes that *psallō* may have meant "play" even in the Bible, but if so then the instrument being played could only be the heart. If one believes that the early church chanted by command of God, then he might hold all of these views and never realize that they contradict one another and that all are foreign to the lexicons.

We have found big differences between English "sing" and Greek "*psallō*." Unlike *psallō* in the first century, our "sing" doesn't have the secondary meaning of strumming on an instrument. The *primary* definitions of these words are *also* distinct in that "sing" is never defined *with* any mention of accompaniment. It's true. You can look in *any* dictionary. Visit used bookstores and libraries. Go online. Consult publishers from Miriam-Webster to Oxford to Funk and Wagnall's; try versions from "Exhaustive" to "International." "Sing" is never defined *with* mention of accompaniment; "*psallō*" is never defined *without* mention of instruments. We must not truncate the meaning of *psallō*; we must not censor the instruments mentioned in *every* lexicon. ***"Psallō" isn't just another word*** for "sing." Again, it is easy to see why the early church never defended their chant by appealing to the meaning of *psallō* as Exclusion does today.

One cannot justify changing praise – forbidding instruments – based on the first century *meaning* of *psallō*. Moreover, *psallō's* primary meaning agrees with John's use of *ōdē* and *ádō* in Revelation. If you were playing charades in the first century, and you wanted to get your friends to say "*psallō*," you would no doubt mimic someone singing and playing an instrument.

## *Psalmos* (the Noun)

*Psalmos* is derived from *psallō*. Here's what the lexicons say about it:

- "psalm" or "song" sung to harp accompaniment.[31]

- ...*the leading idea of* ψαλμ *[psalm] is a musical accompaniment*... [in reference to Colossians 3:16].[32]

- *song sung to the harp, psalm* [citing Ephesians 5:19][33]

- ...later known as the instrument itself, and finally it became known as the song sung with musical accompaniment....[34]

- A song of praise (in the NT probably a reference to an OT psalm)[35]

- ...*song of praise, psalm,* in accordance with OT usage. 1. of the OT Psalms.... 2. of Christian songs of praise [citing 1 Cor 14:26, Eph 5:19, Col 3:16][36]

- The New Testament writers used *psalmos* in two basic senses: first, it refers to the Old Testament psalms, and second, it refers to "songs" of praise and joy....[37]

*Psalmos* occurs 7 times in the New Testament – four times in Luke's writings (Luke 20:42: 24:44: Acts 1:20; 13:33) and three times by Paul (I Corinthians 14:26; Ephesians 5:19; Colossians 3:16). Luke tells us that Christians study the Psalms; Paul tells us that Christians sing psalms. No inspired author says that we are to *only* sing psalms *a cappella*.

## *Humneō* (the Verb)

*Humneō* is Greek for "to sing a hymn" or "to sing the praise of." Of the 6 Greek words for Christian singing, it is the only one not found in either Ephesians or Colossians. It is used of Jesus and the disciples the night of his betrayal (Matthew 26:30 and Mark 14:26), of Paul and Silas in prison (Acts16:25), and of Jesus specifically, in a reference to Psalm 22:22 (Hebrews 2:12).

At Philippi, Paul and Silas are stripped and flogged and then shackled in the prison's inner cell. Unsilenced, the sounds of their prayers and praise fill the prison. It is noteworthy that Luke does not use *psallō* to describe their singing. Perhaps because of *psallō's* instrumental leanings in his day, Luke prefers *humneō* in this context. *Humneō* means to sing praise, regardless of instruments. It is a better word for the singing of Paul and Silas in prison, though it is not a verb that Paul ever uses for *our* singing.

Luke's use of *humneō* does not change its definition to "always *a cappella*" any more than John's use of *ádō* alters the meaning of that word to "always accompanied." Singing *a cappella* once in the Bible doesn't make all singing in the Bible *a cappella*. Rather, this example at Philippi reminds us that the Greek words for singing are different, and that sometimes one suits the given context better than the others. *Psallō* didn't fit at Philippi.

## *Humnos* (the Noun)

*Humnos* is Greek for "a song in praise of gods, heroes, conquerors ... but in the scriptures of God; a sacred song, hymn".[38] The noun occurs only twice in the New Testament (Ephesians 5:19 and Colossians 3:16). In the days of the Apostles, it could be used to refer to the Psalms of David accompanied by instruments.

Josephus (27 – 95 A.D.) designates the psalms of the Old Testament as *humnos*.[39] Here is a sample passage from Josephus cited by Thayer:

> *And now David being freed from wars and dangers, and enjoying for the future a profound peace, composed songs and hymns to God, of several sorts of meter; some of those which he made were trimesters, and*

*some were pentameters. He also made instruments of music, and taught the Levites to sing hymns to God, both on that called the Sabbath day, and on other festivals. Now the construction of the instruments was thus: the viol was an instrument of ten strings, it was played upon with a bow; the psaltery had twelve musical notes, and was played upon with the fingers; the cymbals were broad and large instruments, and were made of brass....* – Antiquities 7.12.3.[40]

This practice was also seen in the Septuagint, where *humnos* refers to the Psalms of David in 2 Chronicles 7:6:[41]

*Thus the king and all the people dedicated the house of God. The priests were standing at their stations, as were the Levites, with the musical instruments of the Lord which David had made for "praising the Lord, for his mercy endures forever," when David used them to accompany the hymns. Across from them the priests blew the trumpets and all Israel stood.* – 2 Chronicles 7:6 (New American Bible)

*Humnos* did not mean "*a cappella* songs" in the days of the Apostles. Neither the lexicons nor the early church make that argument. If "sing means sing" – if *humnos* had only one meaning in all contexts in the first century, then that meaning was not "songs sung *a cappella* <u>only</u>."

## The Meanings of Words

We've looked at three Greek noun-verb pairs for singing. The lexicons say that at least one of them carries the possible implication of instruments. Another was repeatedly used by the Apostle John in the context of worship with accompaniment. All of them are used with instruments in first century contexts of singing. None of them imply *a cappella*. Indeed, **if there is a Greek word for "singing *a cappella*," it isn't in the Bible.**

So, what if you wanted to say "sing with or without instruments" in New Testament Greek? A lot of scholars think that you'd use *ádō* and *psallō*, just like Paul does in Ephesians 5:19. Even Danker concedes that this is the primary first century meaning of *psallō*, and it is consistent with how John uses *ádō* in Revelation.

If you wanted to say "sing and play" in New Testament Greek, how would you do it? A lot of scholars think that you'd say *ádō* and *psallō*, just like Paul does in Ephesians 5:19. Danker acknowledges just a few of them in his lexicon, (though he disagrees with them.) After all, one of the meanings of *psallō* in common usage in the apostles' day was "play," as we have seen. This also agrees with Old Testament usage of the pairing of *ádō* and *psallō* (e.g.: Psalm 57:7 and 108:1).

But what if you wanted to say "sing *a cappella* **only**"? Few scholars think you can get there with *ádō* and *psallō*. It contradicts John's use of *ádō* in Revelation, and it goes against the primary first century meaning of *psallō* in every lexicon. For years we have heard the charge that others are inserting "accompaniment" into the meanings of New Testament Greek words for singing. Upon study, we find that **Exclusion is inserting** "*a cappella* **only**" into those meanings. As we have noted before, the "*a cappella* **only**" camp reaches its conclusion because of its premise that God commanded the early church to chant.

## God's Options

This is a good place to consider an argument made by Jack Lewis, who believes that we should only praise God *a cappella*. In the *Harding University Graduate School of Religion Bulletin*, Lewis writes,

> *It has never been logical to me to argue that the instrument is authorized, but then to argue that its use is optional. Things like water baptism, use of fruit of the vine in the Lord's Supper, and meeting for worship are authorized, but they are not optional.*[42]

Now, no one would be surprised if Lewis argued that God did not authorize praise with instruments, but that is not what he says. He says it is illogical to think that God authorized instruments as optional. He's not saying that God didn't, but that God couldn't.

Again, whenever an argument is puzzling, it may help to consider it as a product of Exclusion's belief that the early church chanted by command of God. When we are told to sing psalms, it is the premise that leads Lewis to mentally discount the instruments in our day as he would similarly disregard a reference to animal sacrifice in our day. As with the nouns, we have seen that none of the New Testament verbs for singing mean *a cappella*. All were used with instruments in the first century. (Indeed, *psallō* may imply instruments, and *ádō* was the choice of the Apostle John to describe accompanied praise.) Because of the premise, however, Lewis cannot imagine the possibility that the scriptures might therefore authorize us to sing, period, regardless of instruments. Instead, the premise leads him to see only two polar options: the authorization to sing only without instruments or the authorization to sing only with instruments. A middle option of "either with or without instruments" (familiar to Old Testament praise) seems hidden from him.

## Borrowing *A Cappella*

"*A cappella*" doesn't look English because it's borrowed from another language, just like *déjà vu* and *per se*. Other languages also borrow from English. Just listen to someone talk about computers in another language, and you'll know it's true! According to Webster's dictionary, *a cappella* joined the English language in about 1864. It came to us from the Italian for "in chapel style."[43] Of course, today it means to sing without instrumental accompaniment.

Its roots are worth noting. Encyclopædia Britannica defines *a cappella* as

> *...performance of polyphonic (multipart) musical work by unaccompanied voices.*[44]

It goes on to explain where the word came from.

> *The a cappella style arose about the time of the composer Josquin dez Prez, in the late 15th century, and reached preeminence with Palestrina in the late 16th century in the music that he wrote for the Sistine Chapel of the Vatican. Because no independent instrumental parts were written, later scholars assumed that the choir sang unaccompanied, but the evidence is now that an organ or other instruments exactly 'doubled' some or several of the vocal parts.*[45]

Josquin dez Perez is respected as one of the greatest composers of all time. He and others of his day began writing music for multiple voices. Perhaps we take the ability to sing that way for granted. I can only imagine what it was like to hear those voices arranged together for the first time. Because this style was rehearsed and made known in church masses of the day, it came to be known as the chapel style.

Truth is stranger than fiction. I would never have imagined a reality so different from what Exclusion teaches about the word, *a cappella*. When I was in high school, our preacher taught that *a cappella* came from the *Latin* language, and that it dated back to how they sang in the early church. He said we sing without instruments because that is the lesson taught by the history of the word "*a cappella*." He was not alone. Instead, we learn that *a cappella* is Italian for a kind of accompanied singing that was in vogue after the Middle Ages – and unknown to the early church. The "chapel" referred to is not the small, quaint house church of the Roman Empire, but rather the likes of the Vatican's Sistine Chapel during the Renaissance. Today the word is primarily known for the part that wasn't true – the absence of accompaniment. There is no God-given mandate to sing only unaccompanied in the history of this word that English has borrowed from Italian.

One wonders why the English language needed a word for "sing without instruments" in 1864. The American Civil War was nearing an end. Churches in the North and South were spitting over slavery, and the Churches of Christ were splitting over slavery *and* instruments.[46] The Bible didn't need *a cappella*, but Exclusion's argument did. Maybe it was only a coincidence, but Exclusion continues to divide the church on behalf of a word that has been passed over for every translation of the Bible.[47] We make "much ado about *a cappella*;" the New Testament does not.

**Were you surprised?** Like me, were you taught that *psallō* once meant either "sing" or "play," but that by the first century it only meant "sing"? Were you surprised like I was to see that its primary first century meaning was a combination of *both* singing and playing – that *psallō* has no English equivalent? Were you surprised that the lexicons which suggest an *a cappella* use of *psallō* are in the minority, and that they limit *psallō*'s meaning in this way *only* in the New Testament, not for linguistic reasons, but for purely religious reasons? Were you surprised that the Apostle John *only* used our words for "sing" in the sense of singing praise with accompaniment? Would you have been the first translator to use the word "*a cappella*" to limit praise?

**Who changed praise?** Sing means "sing," not "sing *a cappella*." The apostle John didn't think that New Testament words for Christians' singing meant *a cappella*. He used *ádō* and *ōdē* (ode) for singing God's praise *with accompaniment* on three different occasions in Revelation. John knew Greek, and he knew worship. None of the other New Testament words for singing conflict with John's usage of *ōdē* and *ádō*. In fact, the primary meaning of *psallō* in the first century was to sing with or without instruments, and its secondary meaning was to play. Neither any apostle nor Jesus himself ever spoke a word against the instruments employed in praising God. John rather gives examples of it.

**Are you missing more than music?** "*A cappella*" is not in the Bible. God never said "*a cappella*," much less "*a cappella* only." The translators have not failed us by declining to use "*a cappella*."

I enjoy attending a congregation where we sing both *a cappella* and accompanied. We have not let go of one to take hold of the other. We are blessed by both. During the week, I also love listening to Christian radio. I often listen in my car and while I work. (There are some very good internet stations for those who live where no Christian radio is on the airwaves.) When I hear a new song that moves me on the radio, I know we can soon sing that new song together in our assemblies. Christian radio exposes us to fresh songs that we can sing more quickly. It helps us appreciate the songs that are moving others. It challenges us through the week. I am thankful that I can turn up the radio.

In these next chapters we'll take a closer look at joy in worship.

---

[1] In the New Testament, accompanied praise is found several times in the Revelation of John. We'll take a look.

[2] Burgess, pp. 81-96.

[3] Thayer, p. 679.

[4] Thayer, p.13. Also, Barth (Botterweck, Theological Dictionary of the Old Testament, vol. IV, p. 93) adds that, "the two meanings 'sing' and 'play' are so firmly linked that is would be more accurate to speak of two aspects of a single meaning: the single action is both 'vocal' and 'instrumental.'" We will see this in John's usage.

[5] In 5:8, John says that the incense of the heavenly creatures, as distinct from their harps and their singing, is symbolic of prayer. (See Psalm 141:2.) Since John doesn't say that either the singing or the instruments are symbolic, Exclusion cannot suggest what the harps or singing might symbolize.

6 John was an Apostle to the Jews (Galatians 2:8, 9).

7 Ferguson, p. 11.

8 Danker, pp. xiv, xv.

9 Ferguson, p. 11

10 Ferguson, p. 13.

11 Ferguson, p. 13.

12 Thayer, 675.

13 Thayer, 637.

14 William F. Arndt and F. Wilbur Gingrich, editors, *A Greek-English Lexicon of the New Testament and other Early Christian Literature*, (based on Walter Bauer's fourth edition, 1952) (Chicago: University of Chicago Press, 1957), p. 899.

15 Henry George Liddell and Robert Scott, compilers, *A Greek-English Lexicon* (Oxford: Clarendon Press, 1968), p. 2018.

16 Gerhard Delling, "Umnos," *Theological Dictionary of the New Testament* (Ann Arbor, Michigan: Cushing p Malloy, Inc., 1972), volume VIII, 493, 494.

17 Delling, pp. 490, 491.

18 Delling, p. 498, footnote 66.

19 Delling, p 499.

20 F. Wilbur Gingrich and Frederick W. Danker, editors, *A Greek-English Lexicon of the New Testament and other Early Christian Literature*, second edition (based on Walter Bauer's fifth edition, 1958) (Chicago: University of Chicago Press, 1979), p. 891.

21 George V. Wingram, *The Analytical Greek Lexicon of the New Testament* (Peabody Massachusetts: Hendrickson Publishers, 1968), p. 441.

22 Johannes P. Louw and Eugene A. Nida, editors, *Greek-English Lexicon of the New Testament based on Semantic Domains,* second edition, (New York: United Bible Societies, 1988), p. 402.

23 *New Testament Greek-English Dictionary,* volume 16 "Sigma to Omega", (Springfield, MO: The Complete Biblical Library, 1991), p. 541.

24 Spiros Zodhiates, *The Complete Word Study Dictionary, New Testament,* (Chattanooga, TN: AMG Publishers, 1992), entry 5567.

25 Frederick William Danker, editor, *A Greek-English Lexicon of the New Testament and other Early Christian Literature*, third edition (based on Walter Bauer's sixth edition), (Chicago: University of Chicago Press, 2000), p. 1096.

26 Ferguson, p. 40.

27 Danker, p. 22. Compare Gingrich and Danker, p.19.

28 Acts 19 tells us that Paul spent 2 and a half years preaching in Ephesus, converting both Jews and Greeks. In time, the local people complained that "large numbers of people" were following Jesus because of the work of Paul (Acts 19: 26).

29 Ferguson, p. 13.

30 R. C. H. Lenski, *The Interpretation of Saint Paul's Epistles to the Galatians, Ephesians, and Philippians* (Minneapolis, MN: Augsburg Publishing House, 1937), p. 620, 621.

[31] James Hope Moulton and George Milligan, *The Vocabulary of the Greek Testament* (London: Hodder and Stroughton, Linited, 1930), p.697.

[32] Thayer, p. 637.

[33] Liddell and Scott, p. 2018.

[34] Zodhiates, entry 5568.

[35] Johannes P. Louw and Eugene A. Nida, editors, *Greek-English Lexicon of the New Testament*, second edition, (New York: United Bible Societies, 1989), p. 402.

[36] Gingrich and Danker, p. 891.

[37] *New Testament Greek-English Dictionary*, p. 542.

[38] Thayer, entry 5212, p. 637

[39] Delling, p. 495. Thayer, entry 5212, p. 637.

[40] Josephus, *The Works of Josephus: New Updated Edition*, Trans. William Whiston (Peabody, Massechusetts: Hendrickson Publishers, 1987), pp. 203-204.

[41] Liddell and Scott, p. 2018.

[42] Dr. Jack P. Lewis, "A Cappella Worship in the Assembly," *Harding University Graduate School of Religion Bulletin*, 39, No. 1 (January 1998), p. 1

[43] *Webster's Ninth New Collegiate Dictionary* (Springfield, Massachusetts: Merriam-Webster Inc., 1987).

[44] *New Encyclopædia Britannica*, vol. 1, (Chicago: Encyclopædia Britannica, Inc., 2005), p. 1.

[45] *New Encyclopædia Britannica*, p. 1.

[46] Milton Jones, *The Other Side of the Keyboard*, Joplin, MO: College Press Publishing Company, 2005, pp. 53-54.

[47] William Tyndale made the first English translation of the Bible, printed in Germany in 1525. For this service, he was burned at the stake as a heretic, but his work served as a basis for English's King James translation in the next century. To make a better translation, Tyndale had *coined* words – like "peacemaker" – but he didn't feel compelled to coin a word for "singing without instruments." Neither has any translator since.

# Praise as it "Once Was" ...and was Prophesied Yet to Be

*All the Levites who were musicians--Asaph, Heman, Jeduthun and their sons and relatives--stood on the east side of the altar, dressed in fine linen and playing cymbals, harps and lyres. They were accompanied by 120 priests sounding trumpets. The trumpeters and singers joined in unison, as with one voice, to give praise and thanks to the LORD. Accompanied by trumpets, cymbals and other instruments, they raised their voices in praise to the LORD and sang: "He is good; his love endures forever."*

*Then the temple of the LORD was filled with a cloud, and the priests could not perform their service because of the cloud, for the glory of the LORD filled the temple of God.* (2 Chronicles 5:12-14)

If you could read that last sentence without being moved, then something is wrong.

In the eyes of Exclusion, this is a throwaway chapter. "It just doesn't matter how God's people 'used to' praise. He may have asked for instruments before, but he hasn't asked for them under the New Covenant." Is Exclusion right?

Did you know that the praise of King David set an example for the Christian praise to come? The Apostle Paul said just that. Writing of *our* praise, Paul cited this prophesy of David, "...as it is written, 'Therefore I will praise you among the Gentiles: I will sing hymns to your name'" (Romans 15:9). What did David foresee? Why did the Spirit lead Paul to cite David as an example for our day? Exclusion argues that the expression of Old Testament praise is virtually immaterial to the discussion of Christian praise. In contrast, Paul says that we are compelled to see what David was talking about when he **prophesied praise for our day**.

To examine the prophecy, this chapter is divided into three parts:
- First, we will take a look at the use of instruments before Jesus came.
- Second, we will study the context of David's prophecy of our praise.
- Finally, we will examine the meaning of David's word for sing in his prophecy.

Let's get started.

## How were Instruments Used Before Jesus Came?

Let's see what we know about Old Testament praise as a backdrop for asking what "sing hymns" to God's name meant when David wrote the prophecy.

1. God desired instruments.

> *He* [Hezekiah] *stationed the Levites in the temple of the LORD with cymbals, harps and lyres in the way prescribed by David and Gad the king's seer and Nathan the prophet; this was commanded by the LORD through his prophets.* (2 Chronicles 29:25)

2. Many of the Psalms specifically mention the instrument(s) played as they are sung.[1]

   Usually it is the lyrics of these psalms that mention the instrument(s) played. About a dozen times, however, although the lyrics don't mention an instrument, still the instrument to be played is found in the psalm's title.[2]

3. Levites used instruments to direct the singing of praise.

   Just over a third of the psalms are addressed (in their titles) to the "Chief Musician" (KJV), "Director of Music" (NIV), or "Choirmaster" (RSV). (See also Habakkuk 3:19.) To understand the role of the "Chief Musician," scholars refer you to 1 Chronicles 15:16, 19-22:

   > [16] *David told the leaders of the Levites to appoint their brothers as singers to sing joyful songs, accompanied by musical instruments: lyres, harps and cymbals....* [19] *The musicians Heman, Asaph and Ethan were to sound the bronze cymbals;* [20] *Zechariah, Aziel, Shemiramoth, Jehiel, Unni, Eliab, Maaseiah and Benaiah were to play the lyres according to alamoth,* [21] *and Mattithiah, Eliphelehu, Mikneiah, Obed-Edom, Jeiel and Azaziah* were ***to play the harps, directing*** *[emphasis mine, DRC; KJV: "to direct with harps"] according to sheminith.* [22] *Kenaniah the head Levite was in charge of the singing [KJV: "was instructor in charge of the music"]; that was his responsibility because he was skillful at it.*

   Those playing musical instruments were said to be "directing" (15:21) the singing.[3] This is the Hebrew word translated "Director of Music" in the titles of 53 psalms.

4. Instrument-playing musicians wrote most of the psalms.

   Asaph, the cymbal-crashing musician to both David and Solomon, was the author of perhaps a dozen Psalms (50, 73 – 83). Korah, whose sons author (or receive?) 11 Psalms (42, 44 – 49, 84, 85, 87, & 88), is referenced in 1 Chronicles 6:22 & 31 as among those "men David put in charge of the music in the house of the Lord, after the ark rested there." David's own name claims about half of the 150 Psalms. Many of the Psalms of these musicians – David,

Asaph, and the sons of Korah – are in turn also entrusted other musicians, to those known as the "Director of Music" … the "Chief Musician."

5. No Old Testament Hebrew word for singing God's praise excluded instruments.

Praise words frequently occur with instruments. As an example, take Psalm 33:1-3, where most of the Hebrew praise words unite in a clear context of instruments.

> *Sing joyfully* (rânan) *to the LORD, you righteous; it is fitting for the upright to praise* (tᵉhillâh, from hâlal) *him. Praise* (yâdâh) *the LORD with the harp; make music* (zâmar) *to him on the ten-stringed lyre. Sing* (shîyr) *to him a new song; play skillfully* (nâgan), *and shout* (tᵉrûw´âh) *for joy (Psalm 33:1-3).*

[As we shall see, the word for "sing" in David's prophecy is *zâmar.*]

6. Even long after David's day, singing praise was associated with instruments.

When Babylon's Jewish captives could not bring themselves to sing (*shîyr*) to God, they hung up their harps. *Shîyr* doesn't mean *play* – it means *sing* – but to these Jews it implied accompaniment. (There is no separate word for "play" in this passage.)

> *By the rivers of Babylon we sat and wept when we remembered Zion. There on the poplars we hung our harps, for there our captors asked us for songs* (shîyr), *our tormentors demanded songs of joy; they said, "Sing* (shîyr) *us one of the songs* (shîyr) *of Zion!" How can we sing* (shîyr) *the songs* (shîyr) *of the LORD while in a foreign land? (Psalm 137:1- 4)*

Ferguson counsels us that *shîyr* "never meant anything but 'sing' in the Hebrew."[4] That much is true, but this passage reminds us not to confuse "sing" with "sing *a cappella.*"

# The Context for David's Prophecy

Now let's take a look at the context surrounding what David said that Jesus would accomplish among us.

> *For I tell you that Christ has become a servant of the Jews on behalf of God's truth, to confirm the promises made to the patriarchs so that the Gentiles may glorify God for his mercy, as it is written:*
> *'Therefore I will praise you among the Gentiles;*
> *I will sing hymns to your name.'* (Romans 15:9)

Scholars say that Paul is quoting King David to the Romans. Paul says that David's praise foretold the impact of Christ's ministry. David hardly *chanted* to God *a cappella*, as they do in the Greek Orthodox Church of today. Let's see what David intended to do among the nations.

Paul is not making an exact quotation from the Old Testament, but David roughly makes this statement on several occasions. One reference is Psalms 57:9 (echoed in Psalm 108:3): "I will praise you, O Lord, among the nations; I will sing of you among the peoples." At the time, did David mean that he would praise God *a cappella*? We don't have to wonder. Here is Psalm 57:7-11 in its context.

> [7] *My heart is steadfast, O God, my heart is steadfast; I will sing and make music.*
> [8] *Awake, my soul! Awake, harp and lyre! I will awaken the dawn.*
> [9] *I will praise you, O Lord, among the nations; I will sing of you among the peoples.*
> [10] *For great is your love, reaching to the heavens; your faithfulness reaches to the skies.*
> [11] *Be exalted, O God, above the heavens; let your glory be over all the earth.*

***David removes all doubt!*** He intended to praise God among the nations on the harp and lyre. (We might note that Psalm 57:7-11 is virtually identical to Psalm 108:1-5, including the instruments specified as being played with David's prophetic verse.[5])

[By the way, Paul alludes to Psalm 57 (and 108) on the topic of singing on another occasion. The call to "*sing and make music*" (Psalm 57:7) is echoed by Paul in Ephesians 5:19. Maybe Paul liked Psalm 57.]

Although no verse matches Paul's quotation exactly, the verse that most closely matches Paul's citation is Psalm 18:49. (Psalm 18 is almost identical to 2 Samuel 22.) Here it reads, "Therefore I will praise you among the nations, O LORD; I will sing praises to your name." This time, David does not identify any instruments. We must ask if David's intent is *a cappella* now and, if so, if Paul then cites this verse to the exclusion of Psalm 57:9. Let's look at the context and the vocabulary to understand what David meant to do in Psalm 18.

Here is a comparison of Psalms 18 and 57.

- Both psalms are committed to the "Chief Musician," a designation for men who led the singing with instruments, as we have already seen. It seems hard to argue that David wrote songs about singing exclusively *a cappella*, and then asked the Levites to lead them with instruments.

- The context of both passages is David's deliverance from Saul, the first king of Israel. From their titles, we learn that Psalm 57 is written when David "fled from Saul into the cave,"[6] while David sings Psalm 18 when God "delivered him from the hands of his enemies and from the hand of Saul." Exclusion has David vowing to praise God with instruments up until his deliverance, when he then uses the same phrase in pledging to praise God only *a cappella*.

- Both Psalm 18:49 and 57:9 unite the Hebrew words *yâdâh* (translated *praise*) and *zâmar* (translated *sing*) together. In the Psalms, this pairing is almost always seen with explicit instruments and/or in psalms directed to the choirmaster.[7] Psalm 57 demonstrates both.

- Psalm 18, unlike Psalm 57, does not identify the instruments by name. However, in *both* prophetic verses, the word translated *sing* is the Hebrew word *zâmar*. What did *zâmar* mean in David's day?

# The Meaning of "Sing" in the Prophecy
## (*Zâmar* among Us, as David Foretold)

The English word *sing* does not occur in the most reliable Hebrew manuscripts. Okay, it doesn't occur in any Old Testament manuscripts. It's English. It's not a word David ever used, not even in his prophecy about our day. The word translated *sing* in his prophecy (in *both* Psalm 18:49 and 57:9) is the Hebrew word *zâmar*. Why did David use *zâmar*? What is its meaning?

You won't find a lexicon that fails to include instruments in defining *zâmar*, David's word of prophecy for our day.

- Strong's dictionary defines *zâmar* as "*To touch the strings* or parts of a musical instrument, i.e. *play* upon it; to make *music*, accompanied by the voice; hence to *celebrate* in song and music."[8] Strong emphasizes playing an instrument, "accompanied by the voice."

- Koehler and Baumgartner give "to play an instrument, to sing" as the primary meaning of *zâmar*, citing Psalm 18:49 specifically as an example.[9]

- In perhaps the most detailed exposition of *zâmar*, C. Barth argues that its *only* meaning is to sing with instruments (along with other forms of praise). He gives three clarifications of that meaning. First, in the spectrum of Hebrew words for praise, *zâmar* falls in the middle and includes shouting and gestures. Second, its instruments encouraged the joy in praise. Third, this praise accompanied by strings is not to be delegated to professionals, but is embraced by everyone, always. See for yourself:

> *IV. Theological Significance. Since* zmr *I is used in OT Hebrew solely in the sense* "sing praises (accompanied by stringed instruments)," *its theological significance is immediately apparent. It can be defined more precisely as follows.*
>
> *1. In the long series of words for hymnic praise,* zmr *occupies a middle position, being a term that covers both articulated praise that speaks in comprehensible words and unarticulated praise*

*expressed in shouts and gestures; through it articulated praise takes on a breadth it does not otherwise exhibit, and unarticulated praise acquires a clarity it otherwise lacks.*

*2. One of the purposes of any hymnic praise is to create and communicate joy; this is especially true for the OT use of* zmr. *Praise expressed in words is all the more productive of joy when sung "accompanied by strings"; praise expressed in instrumental music is more effective when it is sung simultaneously in words, referring explicitly to him in whom true joy has its source.*

*3. The summons to sing Yahweh's praises to the accompaniment of strings is addressed primarily to the assembled congregation and to its assembled members, secondarily, in eschatological prolepsis, to the entire earth. There is no more suggestion that this mandate be delegated to professional singers or musicians than in the case of the summons to praise, glorify, sing, etc. Singing God's praises is fundamentally the function of the devout as a body; they have this joyous mandate – if we may so interpret the exclusive use of the piel – not merely accidentally and occasionally, but habitually, indeed as their profession.* [10]

- Davidson says that *zâmar* means to "sing hymns, praises," often identifying the person celebrated and the instrument for accompaniment.[11]

- The lexicons of Gilbrandt and of Robinson give "making music" as the summary definition, citing both "singing" and "playing."[12] Robinson clearly does not exclude instrumental accompaniment with "sing," because he cites Psalm 57:7 (see 57:8), 71:23 (see 71:22), 98:4 (see 98:5) and 108:1 (see 108:2) as examples of *zâmar* as "sing." Robinson places Psalm 18:49 in the same list of occurrences of "sing."

- Rabin also gives sing and play as definitions of *zâmar*.[13]

Again, you won't find a lexicon that fails to include instruments in defining *zâmar*.

Everything points in the same direction. David praises God in psalm with a word that encompasses singing and playing. At times he even enumerates the instruments he intends to play. These psalms tell how he will praise God this way among the nations. The lexicons specify these citations as examples that include instruments. David commissions these psalms to be led by men who direct them with the playing of instruments. Paul tells us that those psalms are prophetic of New Testament praise. Jesus fulfills David's prophecy, inviting those of use who are not Jews into this experience of praise to God.

What would you see, however, if you had to harmonize these facts with a conviction that the early church chanted by command of God? How could you let David fulfill his pledge to sing among the nations with instruments and yet have Jesus fulfill the prophecy while forbidding them?

Milo Hadwin brings this challenge to his study. In the chapter, "Why do scholars disagree," we saw his assertion that "nothing less than a command of God" could explain the chant of the early church.[14] His approach is to take a second look at the meaning of *zâmar*. We have seen how the lexicons agree in defining *zâmar* as praise that encompassed singing and playing. Several of them say that *zâmar* could even mean to "play" independent of accompanied voice. One lexicon disagrees. Barth thinks that the voice is always included. His definition is "sing praises (accompanied by stringed instruments)." From this definition, Hadwin concludes that *zâmar* had no ties to instruments. He then uses his conclusion from Barth to set aside the instruments in all lexicons. Hadwin writes, "Barth showed from the use of the word [*zâmar*] in the language from which it was borrowed that there is no basis for assigning the meaning of 'play' to the word *zâmar*. This leaves 'sing' as the exclusive meaning of *zâmar*." Hadwin concludes, "It is certain that the word *zâmar* means only 'sing.' It has absolutely no instrumental associations of itself."[15] Every lexicon, including Barth's article, contradicts this conclusion that Hadwin calls "certain." There is no exception. I received permission from Eerdmans Publishing to quote the entire summary of Barth's article in order to show that Barth argued for "instrumental associations" for the word *zâmar*. Hadwin perceives *a cappella* singing in one lexicon and uses that to dismiss all the others. His also dismisses the instruments that David names when he pledges to praise God among the nations. He lets David fulfill his pledge with instruments while having Jesus fulfill David's prophecy without them.

Note that Hadwin does not merely prefer some secondary meaning for *zâmar*; rather, he argues that the primary meaning of *zâmar* in all of the Hebrew lexicons is not a meaning at all. This parallels the attack that Exclusion makes on what the lexicons say is the primary meaning of *psallō* in first century Greek. Its primary meaning is also argued not to be a meaning at all.

Another supporter of only *a cappella* singing takes a different approach to David's prophecy here. Lewis argues that Romans 15:9 "is a reference to what David said he would do (Ps. 18:47-48; 2 Sam. 22:15), not a description of what is done in the church."[16] The defense is puzzling. It seems to say that Paul is citing what David did in his day, prophesied for our day, when no one does the same, at least not in church. It is the kind of conclusion you might reach if you held the conviction that the early church chanted by command of God.

Put another way, these arguments carry the sense that the early church knew something that we don't know, something that would prevent them from praising God with instruments when they saw this prophecy from David. One wonders how the early church knew to exclude instruments without a scripture from God to exclude instruments. Paul knew the Hebrew language well; he was a "Hebrew of Hebrews" (Philippians 3:5). He knew the meaning of *zâmar*, and he knew the setting of David's prophecy. If Paul was intent on eliminating all instruments in the church, it is hard to see how he would cite a verse that explicitly awakens harp and lyre (in Psalms 57 and 108), and yet give no explanation to silence them.

If David wanted to communicate his practice of singing praise to God with words and instruments, he couldn't have chosen a better word than *zâmar*. That's what scholars say it means; that's how it is used. The lexicons of Strong, Koehler, Baumgartner, and Barth expressly say that this is the meaning in Psalm 18:49, and there's no way to get around the instruments of Psalm 57. No lexicon argues that *zâmar* means "*a cappella*" in those passages. Paul cites these words of David as prophetic of singing New Testament praise.

## "Scripture Cannot be Broken" (–Jesus, in John 10:35)

We see what Paul said about David. What did Jesus say about David?

> *"Do not think that I have come to abolish the Law or the Prophets; I have not come to abolish them but to fulfill them. I tell you the truth, until heaven and earth disappear, not the smallest letter, not the least stroke of a pen, will by any means disappear from the Law until everything is accomplished. Anyone who breaks one of the least of these commandments and teaches others to do the same will be called least in the kingdom of heaven, but whoever practices and teaches these commands will be called great in the kingdom of heaven."*
>
> — Jesus (Matthew 5:17-19)

What would we want to be called in the kingdom of heaven? (least or great?)

In this context – in his sermon on the mount – Jesus laid out his view of the Old Testament. In no uncertain terms Jesus reminds us that he came *not* to abolish the law or the prophets, but rather **to *fulfill* them.**

- With a clear understanding of the law and prophets, Jesus condemned not just murder, but hate ... not just adultery, but lust (Matthew 5:21-30).

- With a clear understanding of the law and prophets, Jesus re-focused our giving, our prayer, and our fasting (Matthew 6:1-18).

Jesus shed light on the heart of the law and prophets with regard to *both* our morality *and our service.* And Jesus never breathed a word about excluding clapping or instruments. Jesus came to fulfill prophecy, and one of the prophecies that we KNOW he fulfilled was this prophecy of David. **Jesus came that we Gentiles would know the *zâmar*-song of God. That is what was fulfilled!**

As Jesus said elsewhere of a different Psalm, "Scripture cannot be broken" (John 10:35). Yet without a single "stroke of a pen" in all the

Bible regarding any alteration of the commands to sing and make music (*zâmar*) to God, Exclusion strikes the instruments … and "teaches others to do the same."

## What God Likes

Is it possible that God *likes* instruments? How do you see it? After all, he asked for them, and never spoke any word against them in genuine praise. In defining David's word *zâmar* in the Romans 15:9 prophecy, Barth talked about the joy that instrumental accompaniment brings to songs of praise. A lot of people would agree. Do you have a button on your car radio set to an *a cappella* music station? …Only if you have satellite radio. Powerful words set to music reach to our core; instruments impact. God knows what he is doing.

Exclusion says that believers only praise with instruments because it's what *we* like. It asserts that instruments are *not* what *God* likes. Uncooperatively, the Bible never makes those arguments. It is difficult indeed to argue that God dislikes what he asked for and what he prophesied for us.

Romans 15:9 reminds us that David had praised God's name and had sung to him among the Gentiles, and that it was always God's intent that we Gentiles praise and sing to his name. Christ's work brought final fulfillment to David's prophecy. The goal was that you and I might "glorify God for his mercy." Without Christ's work, we would be "without hope and without God in the world" (Ephesians 2:12). Lest we get too caught up and distracted by questions of instruments or how many people must sing along with me, let us thank God that we *do* glorify Him for his work in us. Christ did that for us, and David foresaw it. **Christ brought *us* the *zâmar*-praise of God.**

By the way, if no passage of scripture prophesied the end of praise *with* instruments, neither does any scripture prophesy the end of praise *without* instruments. Under the Old Covenant, God's people praised him with and without accompaniment. He was pleased with both. God liked both.

*Were you surprised?* I had heard that David "invented" instruments in worship. Instead, were you surprised to see God communicate his desire for accompanied praise through numerous prophets? Were you surprised that most psalmists were instrument-playing musicians, and that the chief musicians led singing with their instruments? (They had no P.A. system!) Do any of the scholarly efforts to interpret David's prophecy as strictly *a cappella* for our day satisfy you?

***Who changed Praise?*** God asked for musical instruments. David didn't change this; he praised God with instrumental accompaniment. By inspiration, he prophesied the same praise for us. Paul didn't change it; he reminded us of David's prophecy for our day. Jesus didn't change praise; he fulfilled the whole prophecy. **Did any inspired writer change praise?** Do you wish that Paul had cited some other verse, as though this "confusion" were *his* fault? What do you make of the "harp and lyre" that David prophesied would be played in praise among the nations because of Jesus?

***Are you missing more than music?*** Understand the joy intended in every breath of David's praise. "Praise as it once was" was a praise that expressed joy! Make that joy a standard for *your* praise. Christ brought *us* a joyful celebration of song. Let it escape with shouts and clapping. Don't be afraid to jump for joy, like a small child at VBS. Lift up holy hands. In your non-Christian songs, if you are moved by a driving drum beat or the crescendo of a symbol, if you turn up the volume to hear the base guitar and shout with the lead singer, then let that same passion invade your praise to God. Make a joyful noise to the Lord, all the earth!

David praised with this kind of joy. Absolutely! Because of Christ, he foresaw the same for us. Fill yourself up with joy so the prophecy is fulfilled in you.

---

[1] 4:T (Title); 5:T; 6:T; 8:T; 12:T; 33:2; 43:4; 49:4; 54:T; 55:T; 57:8; 61:T; 67:T 68:25; 71:22; 76:T; 81:T, 2; 84:T; 87:7; 92:3; 98:5; 108:2; 137:2; 144:9; 147:7; 149:3; and 150:3, 4, & 5; Gesenius adds 45:T; 53:T; 69:T; and 80:T [*Gesenius' Hebrew and Chaldee Lexicon to the Old Testament Scriptures,* trans. Samuel Prideaux Tregelles (Grand Rapids, MI: Baker Book House, 1979), p. 562].

[2] Jesus (Mark 12:35-37), Peter (Acts 1: 15-20; 2:25-28, 29-35), and Paul (Romans 4:6-7; 11:9-10) affirm psalm titles when presenting arguments from the Old Testament. Regarding the titles to the Psalms, we should note that "there are no Hebrew manuscripts, however ancient, without them." Albert Barnes, *Notes on the Old Testament.* (Grand Rapids, MI: Baker Book House, 1950), *Psalms, Vol. 1,* p. xvii.]

[3] *Gesenius,* p. 562; J. M. Cook, *The Bible Commentary; I Samuel – Esther* (Grand Rapids, Michigan: Baker Book House, 1953), p. 345.

[4] Ferguson, p. 6.

[5] I emphasize Psalm 57 because Psalm 108 is entirely an arrangement from two other psalms – opening with Psalm 57:7-11, followed immediately by Psalm 60:5-12. Incidentally, Psalms 57 and 60 are both committed to the director of music.

[6] The title of this psalm tells us that David wrote it "When he had fled from Saul into the cave." Twice the Bible mentions David fleeing from Saul into caves. In 1 Samuel 22:1 & 2, 400 men join David. The number grows to 600 (23:13), and they again enter a cave (24:3) in flight from Saul. David praises God among these men ... in a cave ... on the harp and lyre. And he continues to praise God in this way beyond the confines of these caves. He says so.

[7] *yâdâh* with *zâmar* (1) with explicit instruments: **33**:2; **57**:8, 9; **71**: 22, 23; **92**:1-3; **108**:2, 3; (2) commissioned to the director of music: **9**:1,2; **18**:49; **57**:9; **105**:1,2 (For Psalm 105, see 1 Chronicles 16:7), and (3) without direct mention of instruments: **30**:4, 12 (Title: for the dedication of the temple) and **138**:1 (of David).

[8] James Strong, "A Concise Dictionary of the Words in the Hebrew Bible," *The New Strong's Exhaustive Concordance of the Bible.* (Nashville: Thomas Nelson Publishers, 1984 (orig. 1890)), p. 35.

[9] Ludwig Koehler and Walter Baumgartner, *The Hebrew and Aramaic Lexicon of the Old Testament,* (New York: E. J. Brill, 1994), pp. 273-274. Other meanings offered are (2) "to praise" (citing Psalm 57:9), (3) "to sing, praise" (citing Psalm 57:7), and (4) "to play an instrument." It is clear that the authors do not understand the meanings "praise" or "sing" to be expressly *a cappella*, since the verses they site for those meanings from Psalm 57 sandwich verse 8, where instruments are absolutely specified. These scholars see neither Psalm 18:49 nor 57:9 as *a cappella*.

[10] C. Barth, *"Zâmar"* Botterweck, G. Johannes and Ringgren, Helmer, editors, *A Theological Dictionary of the Old Testament,* (Grand Rapids, Michigan: William B. Eerdmans Publishing Company, 1980), Volume IV, 98.

[11] Benjamin Davidson, *The Analytical Hebrew and Chaldee Lexicon* (Grand Rapids, Michigan: Zondervan Publishing House, 1970 (orig. work 1848)), p. 239. He does not indicate that it failed to be a song of praise if the "person celebrated" is omitted nor that it implied *a cappella* whenever no instrument is specified.

[12] Thoralf Gilbrant, editor, *Old Testament Hebrew-English Dictionary* (Springfield, MO: World Library Press Inc., 1996), volume Gimel-Zayin, p. 2252.; Edward Robinson, ed., *A Hebrew and English Lexicon of the Old Testament* by William Gesenius (Oxford: Clarendon Press, 1953 (orig 1907)), p.274.

[13] Haim Rabin, *A Comprehensive Etymological Dictionary of the Hebrew Language for Readers of English* (New York: MacMillan Publishing Company, 1987), p. 200.

[14] Hadwin, p. 55.

[15] Milo Richard Hadwin, "Chapter 4. What Kind of Music Does God Want?" Sheerer, Jim and Williams, Charles L., editors, *Directions for the Road Ahead: Stability in Change Among the Churches of Christ,* (Chickasha, Okla.: Yeoman Press, 1998), p. 63

[16] Jack P. Lewis, Everett Ferguson, and Earl West, *The Instrumental Music Issue,* Nashville, TN: The Gospel Advocate Co., 1987, p. 43.

# Why Would God Nail "David's Praise" to the Cross?

If the era of accompaniment in praise has ended, then the follow-up question that many want to ask is, "Why?" Why did God change his position on instruments? (Or, why did he ever *want* them?) Why did God nail "David's praise" to the cross? Exclusion is curious for answers, too. Conceding that the Bible never tries to *justify* the abolition of accompaniment in New Testament praise, Exclusion nevertheless offers reasons for the change. In this chapter, let's look at "David's praise" and at Exclusion's insight on *why* God ended it. We begin with another prophecy of praise given by inspiration to David.

In this next prophecy of Praise, David spoke about how Jesus himself would praise. As David praised, so would Jesus. You see, the writer of Hebrews says that David was speaking of Jesus when he wrote,

*I will declare your name to my brothers; in the presence of the congregation I will sing your praises.* (Hebrews 2:12).

The quotation comes from Psalm 22:22. The entire psalm, written by David, is widely acknowledged as prophetic of Jesus. You can clearly identify the quotation from verse 22:

*I will declare your name to my brothers; in the congregation I will praise you.*

This chapter asks not *if*, but *why* God would oppose instruments. As we shall see, Exclusion argues that instruments are (1) unspiritual, (2) an Old Testament shadow, and (3) tied up with a desire for entertainment. Before we examine those arguments, let's first take a look at David, because he made this prophecy, and because no name comes to mind ahead of his on the subject of praising God in song. First we'll look at the Hebrew word for praise that David uses in this prophecy and how he and the kings who followed him used it. Then, against this backdrop of David, we will be ready to examine Exclusion's scholarly arguments against instruments in the fulfillment of David's prophecy.

## David's Celebration of Praise

What did David prophesy that Jesus would do in the congregation? The Hebrew word for "praise" in this passage hardly means, "Be still and chant." The Hebrew word for "praise" prophesied in Psalm 22:22 is *hâlal*. Its primary meaning is to sing praise, to celebrate.[1] Let's look at how it was used.

*Hâlal*-praise is called for in 33 psalms.[2] Psalm 150 calls for *hâlal*-praising God with seven different musical instruments, and Psalms 149:3 and 150:4 call for *hâlal*-praising God with dancing. Most of David's *hâlal*-psalms, including Psalm 22, are commissioned to the "director of music" – those Levites who directed with musical instruments, as we have seen.

Just as the psalms told believers _to_ *hâlal*-praise God, so the Chronicles tell us _how_ they *hâlal*-praised him. When David decreed *hâlal*-praise (1 Chronicles 16:4, 5; 23:5; and 25:3), he commanded instruments, and the kings after him followed his lead. Let's look at the first time that David commanded *hâlal*-praise in 1 Chronicles.

In 1 Chronicles 15, Israel is bringing the ark to Jerusalem. David leads the people as they praise God with shouts, rams horns and trumpets, cymbals, lyres and harps, dancing, and great joy (15:19, 20). When they reach Jerusalem, David immediately appoints Levites to *hâlal*-praise God, specifying lyres and harps, cymbals, and trumpets to be played regularly before the ark (16:4-6), according to each day's requirements (16:36, 37).[3] "Then all the people left, each for his own home, and David returned to bless his family" (16:43). 2 Samuel 6:20-23 tells us that when David reached home that day, his wife Michal confronted him over the way he praised God. It was perhaps the first split over worship.

It is rare to find *hâlal* described in the Chronicles under *any* king without the specification of instruments.[4] 2 Chronicles 7:6 and 30:21 say that *hâlal*-praising was done with the "Lord's instruments." (Similarly, in his Revelation, John says that the martyrs praise with "harps of God.") *Hâlal*-praise was a bold celebration; it was never timid.

Can you picture Jesus *hâlal*-praising God the way David did? Can you picture Jesus joining in a celebration of praise that included musical instruments (or dancing)? Can you see Jesus praising God boldly, the way David prophesied that he would?

Exclusion cannot. "But even if Jesus *did hâlal*-praise God," Exclusion answers, "then he did so under the *Old* Covenant. *Hâlal* was authorized (or at least tolerated) under the *Old* Covenant, but there is no example of this kind of praise under the *New* Covenant. Jesus' *hâlal*-praising days were nailed to the cross. Early Christians sat or stood and chanted, and we should be still and sing only *a cappella* today."

Now we are ready to look at several reasons given by Exclusion for nailing "David's praise" to the cross.

## 1. Was David's Praise Unspiritual?

Exclusion believes that *hâlal*-praise ceased because *a cappella* singing alone is "spiritual." Ferguson says, "There is a real question whether the offering of instrumental music is consistent with the spiritual nature of Christian worship. As a mechanical act, producing instrumental music is distinct from the offering of spiritual worship, that is, what comes from the spiritual nature of man."[5] (Note the word "mechanical.") Exclusion asserts that Jesus took "unspiritual" instruments and dancing with him to the grave.

David claims to sing and make music (on the harp and lyre) with "all my soul" (Psalm 108:1). Exclusion contradicts him, saying that in fact you can*not* play an instrument in praise with "all your soul." Do you think David praised God as he said with *all* his soul?

The New Testament agrees that it is not vocal chords that make an offering of song spiritual. God rejects lip service. Paul reminds us to engage our "hearts" when we (like David) "sing and make music." (Compare Eph. 5:19 with Psalm 108:1.) Worship that fails to engage our hearts and souls defines unspiritual worship.

Misunderstanding this, some have argued that the prophet Amos condemned accompaniment in praise (Amos 5:23; 6:5). They blame the instruments that God asked for. Reading these verses in context finds God rejecting *all* the service of these people – their sacrifices as well as their songs – because their hearts and souls were far from him. The problem was with hypocrisy – with unspiritual people, not with "unspiritual" instruments. God would not have been pleased with hypocrites if they had only praised him *a cappella*! In the same way, Ezekiel condemned the prayers of the hypocrite (Ezek. 8:18), but that doesn't make prayer itself unspiritual. In truth, the only time that the prayers or accompanied praise of the *righteous* are <u>ever</u> called unacceptable is from the lips of the *unrighteous*, from those like Michal.

The Bible identifies David as the "man after God's own heart,"[6] and it NEVER says that he established *unspiritual* praise! After a thousand years, Jesus did not come to take his stand with Michal. He did not agree with her that David's praise was second rate. Exclusion thinks that when Jesus died, he ended the age of David's "unspiritual" celebration, but NO VERSE OF SCRIPTURE ever questions the spiritual nature of the praise given to David by command of God. When Exclusion alleges that instrumental music or clapping are "unspiritual," it is not "speaking where the Bible speaks."

## 2. Did David Sing Praise with Shadows?

We know that some aspects of Old Testament worship were a "shadow" of what Christ was to bring (Hebrews 10:1). He fulfilled the sacrifice for sin, replacing the shadow of animal blood with the reality of his own. David offered animal sacrifices for sin, but we do not. We dare not. The perfect sacrifice for sin has since been offered.

Exclusion argues that the instruments of song in the old law were a shadow like animal sacrifices, and that we *also* dare not use *them*. Ferguson writes, "Instruments of Music belonged to the childhood of the human race's spiritual development. They appealed to the senses and have been abolished from the Christian assemblies with the other types and shadows of the Old Testament."[7]

Unlike animal blood, however, instruments are **nowhere** called a shadow. Nowhere are we told that the *need* for instruments was satisfied by Christ's work. Nowhere are we told *what* they may have shadowed or what may have replaced them. David did not praise God with instruments because man was somehow not yet worthy to praise God *a cappella*. Jesus' death did not open the door to *a cappella* singing. Indeed, the Old Testament children of Abraham already praised God with and without instruments. David did not sing praise with anything that the Bible calls a shadow. Without a word from God, what we dare not do is declare instruments a shadow. With no word from God, we dare not abolish the prophecies of *hâlal* and *zâmar*, and forbid them.

The problem with this argument is further compounded when it is made together with the first argument. It is one thing to say that instruments were either unspiritual or a shadow; it is quite another to say that instruments were both. By alleging that instruments were both a shadow *and* unspiritual, Exclusion's scholars create a special class for instruments, for nothing else in all the Bible is labeled as both. The shadow of animal sacrifices, for example, is never called unspiritual. Indeed, Paul tells us that it is *we* who were unspiritual, *not* God's law (Romans 7:14). His "shadows" were not unspiritual. If one were convinced that the early church chanted by command of God, then he might not see that these arguments contradict not only the Bible, but also each other.

## 3. That's Entertainment!

If David's praise is labeled as "unspiritual" by Exclusion, so it is also scorned as "entertainment." It is called not merely a shadow, but a show.

Exclusion often contends that believers who play instruments, lift hands, or sing solos are only trying to entertain others or draw attention to themselves. Of course, **there's no passage equating this kind of praise with entertainment.** Rather, Exclusion's argument would make God himself the *author* of this kind of "entertainment" in the Old Testament by virtue of his commandments. Is God now put off by the "entertainment" that he required in the Old Testament? By this logic, Exclusion's argument makes David an entertainer set on drawing attention to himself … and that, by commandment of God.

That is what Michal thought. She saw her husband, David, publicly remove his outer garment, dancing freely before the Lord. She "despised" David (2 Samuel 6:16) and met him at the door to denounce the spectacle he had made of himself (6:20). David answered that her pitiful attitude was the same as that of her father Saul – whose stance had led to his removal as king of Israel. Regarding his "spectacle" of praise, David concluded by saying, "You ain't seen nothin' yet!" (6:21-22, my paraphrase, DRC).

We must learn from Michal, and take care about *our* attitude … and our accusations.

## 4. The Lesser of Two Evils (obsolete)

The first Christians to condemn instruments in worship, as we have seen in the chapter on the chant, lived in the fifth century. Just as they did not condemn instruments for the same reasons as Exclusion today, neither does modern Exclusion condemn instruments for the reason that they gave. In the chapter on the chant, we saw that they condemned instruments as evil. It is inherently difficult to label instruments as evil after Calvary without casting them as evil before it. The fifth century opponents saw the difficulty and faced it head on. David's instruments, too, they said, were evil. More precisely, instruments were the lesser of two evils. God chose to let David and others worship him with evil instruments rather than to risk David not worshipping him at all, they thought. Modern Exclusion distances itself from its fifth century forerunners; Exclusion will not call David's instruments evil. Exclusion says that instruments are unspiritual, but only in our day. It disputes that they were evil or unspiritual in David's day.

If you believe that the early church chanted by command of God, then you do not see the contradictions. Exclusion is not concerned that modern arguments opposing instruments do not match those of fifth century Christians who first opposed instruments. Exclusion discards their charge – that instruments were evil, even in the hands of David. Exclusion can say that instruments are unspiritual and showy today, while granting that they were not in David's hands. Exclusion can go on to label instruments as both unspiritual and a shadow today, disregarding the fact that God's shadows were quite spiritual. Over all of this is the contradiction that the Bible itself never makes any of these charges against instruments in New Testament worship.

The Bible never tells us *that* God changed his mind about instruments, so it certainly does not suggest *why* he might have changed his mind. Exclusion deduces not only the change, but also the reasons for it. However, the scriptures confirm that David's praise wasn't unspiritual and shallow, and it wasn't a shadow or a mere show. It certainly was not evil. Jesus didn't nail David's praise to the cross, and its author wasn't David. The same inspiration that lead *David* to celebrate God in praise foretold that *Jesus* would celebrate God in praise. And Jesus did.

**Jesus didn't die to *still* David's praise; he came to *fulfill* David's prophecies.** Watch your youth at VBS. You can praise God with your feet on the floor and your hands to your side, but Jesus didn't die to nail them there!

## A *Cappella*-Colored Vocabulary

Professional communicators know that one's choice of words is extremely important in persuasion. For example, should Planned Parenthood be painted as pro-choice or pro-abortion? Is the immigration debate about "illegal aliens" or "undocumented workers"? If a print article or poll question is framed with words that elicit strong emotions, it often gets a different response from the same presentation without the loaded vocabulary. It is easier to get the response you want if you use the vocabulary most favorable to your cause.

We began these chapters on musical instruments with the observation that Exclusion teaches us to praise God with vocabulary that the Bible never uses. Exclusion rather brings its own vocabulary – "*a cappella*", "congregational singing", "corporate worship", "mechanical instruments." Unfortunately for all of us, that vocabulary is emotionally charged. Consider this common question from Exclusion: "Since the New Testament never mentions 'mechanical instruments in corporate worship,' how can we approve of them?" Exclusion's use of vocabulary that is foreign to the Bible may sway you to answer this question in agreement with those who oppose musical accompaniment. But consider an opposing question: "Since the New Testament never mentions '*a cappella*, congregational singing,' how can we require it alone in 'corporate worship' alone?" This question draws out a different response. The debate turns on Exclusion's vocabulary rather than on the vocabulary of the inspired writers.

Though the Bible never mentions *a cappella*, it has much to say about musical instruments. It just never says what Exclusion says about them. God never says they were unspiritual. God never says they were a shadow. By introducing the extra-Biblical phrase "mechanical instruments," Exclusion subtly introduces concepts which are equally foreign to the Bible. Exclusion prejudices the debate by arguing with vocabulary that is unknown to the Bible, loaded with emotions from 100 years of hurt. If we are not careful, we become slaves to vocabulary that does not teach what the Bible says.

When we set aside the vocabulary that is not found in the Bible, we open ourselves to the perspective of the vocabulary that *is* there. Removing the *a cappella*-colored vocabulary allows us to remove the *a cappella*-colored glasses. We have seen that the Bible tells us to "sing and make music," a phrase which Bible translators say they use to embrace accompaniment, spanning the Old Testament (Psalms 57, 108, etc.) and the New (Ephesians 5:19). We have found that the New Testament uses the vocabulary of accompanied praise, cites prophecies of accompanied praise, and gives examples of accompanied praise. Replacing the Bible words for "sing" with "*a cappella* only (in the context of corporate worship alone)" contradicts the writings of everyone else in the first century, from the Apostle John in the New Testament, to Josephus outside of it. Others today are not adding "accompaniment" to the Bible's vocabulary; Exclusion rather is replacing the Bible's vocabulary with its own.

**Were you surprised?** When Michal confronted David, he didn't quote her a verse for removing his outer garment. Were you surprised by his answer? Did you raise an eyebrow when inspiration referred to "the Lord's instruments"? Exclusion's scholars say that Old Testament accompanied worship was unspiritual and a shadow. Were you surprised that no scripture says so or gives *any* reason *why* God would have changed his mind about praise?

**Who changed praise?** Who said that instruments were nailed to the cross? Where is it written that instruments offer "unspiritual" worship? Where in the New Testament are instruments called a shadow? Who said that instruments were undignified or based on the desire to entertain or draw attention? Exclusion makes these charges with no scriptural support. Nowhere does the Bible attempt to *justify* the end of instruments. The Bible never argues that style of praise given to David (and others) was nailed to the cross; it rather prophesies more of the same.

**Are you missing more than music?** Have you witnessed worship in song that would parallel the heart of David? Have you seen passion for praise that could not be contained? In the last chapter, one scholar pointed out how instruments contribute to that kind of joy in praise. I cannot explain it, but I know that praise with accompaniment often finds me shedding tears of joy. That was not my experience when I sang only, always *a cappella*.

David desired to unleash worship; Michal wanted to tame it. Scripture has taken its stand with David. Therefore, we cannot let today's Michals intimidate and silence us. God never looks down his nose if you sing off key. Your song *is* good enough. Don't let men reduce your praise to a performance to be judged or approved by them. Falling on your knees is "undignified." Praising like David is "undignified" (1 Samuel 6:22). Forget stale dignity. Praise to please God; Michal cannot be pleased.

Some are not comfortable praising like David. That's okay. We just can't make it our mission to stop David, like Michal tried to do. She's not a good role model.

---

[1] Gesenius, entry 1984, page 226.
[2] David is identified as the author of 13 of the *hâlal* psalms, including Psalm 22, and he may have written some of the others as well. David *hâlal*-praises God in **18**:3; **22**:22, 23, 26; **34**:2; **35**:18; **56**:4, 10; **63**:5, 11; **64**:10; **69**:30, 34; **96**:4; **105**:3,

45; **106**:1, 5, 48; **109**:30; and **145**:2, 3. He is identified as the author of Psalms 96; 105:1-15; and 106:1, 47, 48 – where we find most of the occurrences of *hâlal* of these 3 psalms – in I Chronicles 16:7-36; verse 7 adds that these psalms were also commissioned to the musician Asaph. The other psalms on David's list are attributed to him in their titles, where all but 34, 35, 63, and 145 are committed to the chief musician. The other *hâlal*-praise psalms are **44**:8; **48**: 1; **74**:21; **84**:4; **102**:18; **104**:35; **107**:32; **111**:1; **112**:1; **113**:1, 3, 9; **115**:17, 18; **116**:19; **117**:1, 2; **119**:164, 175; **135**:1, 3, 21; **146**:1, 2, 10; 147:1, 12, 20; **147**: 1, 12, 20; **148**:1-7, 13, 14; **149**:1, 3, 9; and **150**:every verse.

3 *Hâlal* occurs more often in 1 Chronicles 16 (verses 4, 10, 25, 36) than it does in any other chapter of the Bible, with the exception of Psalms 149 and 150.

4 Besides 1 Chronicles 16, instruments are specified in describing *hâlal* in 1 Chronicles 23:5; 25:3; 2 Chron. 5:13; 7:6; 23:12,13; 29:25-30; and 30:21. 2 Chron 8:14 and 31:2 don't mention instruments, but speak of Levites "praising" God according to their "duties." Only once, in 2 Chron. 20:19, 21 is *hâlal* observed without mention of instruments or duties.

5 Ferguson, p. 88.

6 1 Samuel 13:14; Acts 13:22

7 Lewis, Ferguson, and West, p. 109.

Exclusion's Fourth
Disputable Matter:

"The New Testament is Silent
on Singing or Listening to Solos"

# When Listening to Praise is a Sin

High school graduation marks an exodus for many of our children. Away from home in a new town, they ask themselves what kind of church they are looking for, if for one at all. Many leave church entirely. Others quietly leave the Churches of Christ in search of something they see as "more spiritual." They aren't seeking instruments; they seek the presence of God. Campus ministers see it every fall. Our churches are perplexed to have such difficulty attracting these young singles. We offer them programs to get involved in, but they aren't anxious to plug into our programs. If children are to be seen and not heard, they are no longer children. They want to hear and share what God is doing around us, but our assemblies are already programmed. They sense that we just want them so we can count them.

Those who want to leave but stay are apt to find themselves among those at the back of the assembly. Have you ever sat back there and noticed how many people barely sing ... and how many rarely sing? It doesn't seem to matter whether instruments are used or not. We scratch our heads and wonder why so many are convinced that their voices are unnecessary. We want them to join our song. We make "every effort" to turn the tide and bring their voices in. We offer them only the best "worship leaders." We give additional microphones to talented singers so that everyone can follow along with his or her part. We amplify voices (rather than instruments) until the song swells ... except in the rear.

This chapter takes a look at the difference between wanting to hear others sing *our* song and yearning to hear *their* song – the song God has given them. This chapter has four sections. First, we will lay out Exclusion's teaching that singing is the lone service offered in our assemblies which must only be done "congregationally," or in unison. Second, we will examine the meaning of the phrase "one another" to see if it commands only simultaneous action only in contexts of singing. Third, we will compare singing in our assemblies with the New Testament outline. Finally, we will compare our singing with the Old Testament outline for the temple. Let's begin with the distinctive rule for "congregational" singing in our assemblies.

## Different Rules Only for Singing

Exclusion teaches that the New Testament ushered in another change to our singing: Before Jesus came, you could listen to the praise in song of another believer (from Miriam in Exodus 15:20, 21 to Mary in Luke 1:46-55),[1] but not any more. Exclusion's new rules for singing are different from the rules for all other worship offered to God.

Have you noticed?

- In our assemblies, we can listen to a **prayer**, and our worship is acceptable. But if anyone *sings* that same prayer, then our worship is no longer acceptable ... unless we sing along.

- We can listen as **scripture** is read, and our worship is accepted. But if anyone *sings* those same verses, then our worship is abruptly unacceptable ... unless we join in, audibly.

- We can listen to **praise** offered for what God has done, and our worship is acceptable. But if anyone *sings* that same testimony, then our worship ends ... unless we know those words and speak them.

- We can hear the **lyrics** to a song quoted, and our worship is acceptable. But if anyone *sings* those same stanzas, then our worship is no longer acknowledged ... unless we sing, too.

Exclusion has determined that in Christian assemblies **all singing must be "congregational."** Since that **language occurs nowhere in the Bible**, it must be explained. By "congregational singing," Exclusion means that *everyone* must sing whenever *anyone* sings. Exclusion does not teach exclusively *"congregational"* praying (where everyone raises their voice at the same time),[2] or exclusively *"congregational"* scripture reading or exclusively *"congregational"* preaching. In fact, the only time Exclusion deduces the "congregational" mandate, requiring that everyone "speak" or "teach and admonish" all at once, in unison, is *every* time words are set to music.

Let's see what Biblical evidence there is for making our songs different from all other service.

## Same Song, Second Verse

Exclusion's arguments against listening to a believer (or to a group of believers) share a song of praise echo the arguments against instruments.

- Nowhere does the Bible say that God has changed his mind about believers listening to praise or prayer or teaching or scripture … only when it is sung.

- Nowhere does the Bible explain *why* God would change his mind about believers listening to praise or prayer or teaching or scripture … only when it is sung.

- The **vocabulary** for our singing is the same in the two testaments, but Exclusion interprets all of the singing contexts to mean "congregational" only in the New Testament.

- The arguments against active listening are "**deduced**" from passages about our daily lives, yet they are applied in a different, restricted context, only to assemblies.

- Neither *"a cappella"* nor "congregational" are in the Bible.

The basis for Exclusion's argument lies squarely in the meaning of "one another" in Ephesians 5:19 and Colossians 3:16. Let's take a look.

# Sing to Yourselves
## (Even When You're All Alone)

To get started, let's take a moment to consider what we might learn from these passages if we were not focused so intently on *our* issues. In an earlier chapter, we saw how Ephesians 5 and Colossians 3 are written about our lives in general, not just our lives during assemblies, and certainly not during assemblies only. What then could we learn from these passages with regard to our daily lives? And what about those times when we are all alone?

These next few paragraphs examine an aspect of praise that is overlooked when we make Ephesians 5 apply only to praise in our assemblies. Yes, "sing to yourselves" in Ephesians 5:19 has something to say about whether or not we may listen to another sing a solo, but "sing to yourselves" also has implications beyond our debate. These next few paragraphs have no final significance in that debate over solos, but please don't skip them. A couple of big words – reflexive and reciprocal – might be enough to scare you off as well. Still, there is a payoff. These paragraphs give some food for thought about how we talk to ourselves during the day. They give us a glimpse of praise beyond the debate over solos.

To avoid the accusation of comparing apples to oranges, we should note that the verbs in Ephesians 5:19 ("speak to one another") and Colossians 3:16 ("teach and admonish one another") are actually reflexive verbs ("to yourselves") seen as reciprocal verbs ("to one another"). What's the difference? Well, if I told my sons to "wash your hands" for dinner, you'd think that I meant for each son to wash his own hands (reflexive). You wouldn't expect them to wash each other's hands (reciprocal).

In the same way, when a group is addressed with a reflexive verb in the New Testament the thought is *typically* to do something to or for yourself, NOT to or for "one another." For example, "offer **yourselves** to God" (Romans 6:13) doesn't mean that we should offer one another to God (reciprocal), but that each should offer himself (reflexive). Similarly, "consider others better than **yourselves**" (Philippians 2:3) means that each should consider others better than himself (reflexive). It doesn't even make sense to translate this reciprocally: "Consider others better than one another." There are numerous examples of second person plural ("y'all do this") reflexive verbs in the New Testament.[3] Although there are exceptions, they are typically translated with "yourselves" and mean something that each in the group does to or for himself.

Again, the Greek verbs in Ephesians 5:19 ("speak to one another") and Colossians 3:16 ("teach and admonish one another") are actually reflexive verbs. Because of that, some believe that this reflexive sense is indeed the main intent of Ephesians 5:19.[4] In that light, the passage would read that a Christian shouldn't be filled with alcoholic spirits (5:18), but should be filled with the Holy Spirit, speaking to himself in psalms, etc. (5:19) This fits with "self-talk" passages like Philippians 4:8. The KJV renders Ephesians 5:19 as "speaking to yourselves in psalms…" where most modern translations say "speaking to one another…" If this reflexive sense is one way to look at Eph. 5:19, then it is real affirmation for all of you who sing to yourselves in the shower (reflexive, of course)! We all enjoy singing "to one other," but even when we're alone, we can sing "to ourselves" in psalms, hymns, and spiritual songs. Do you do that? During the week, are you often found singing secular songs, or songs of God's faithfulness? It will be a lot easier to be "filled with the Spirit" if you're not waiting until you can get up a group on Sunday to sing songs of praise.

Well, anyway, the meaning doesn't have to be reflexive. All scholars recognize that Greek reflexive verbs sometimes take on a reciprocal ("one another") meaning. Many (most?) believe that this is the case in Ephesians 5:19 and Colossians 3:16. Moulton and Geden identify 17 examples of reflexive verbs (a small minority of the whole) that they believe are used as reciprocals, including our two verses.[5] Half of their examples are in the second person plural (yourselves). Let's learn from them.

# The "Simultaneous" Flaw: I Can't Sing Without You

As we look at these other "one another" passages (all reflexive verbs used as reciprocal verbs), keep an eye out for Exclusion's necessary addition. Exclusion argues that the "one another" activity of Eph 5:19 and Col 3:16 (singing to "one another") must be done *simultaneously... congregationally.* These verses are said to teach that if one Christian sings, everyone else *must* sing, too. Let's see if that's what "one another" means.

Granted, some "one another" practice is really an attitude that never stops. "Be at peace among yourselves" (I Thess. 5:13). "Love one another deeply" (I Peter 4:8). But other "one another" activity (like singing) is not a ceaseless attitude, but an action:

- **As each one has received a gift, minister it to one another** (I Peter 4:10). If you and I both have a ministry of teaching, this passage teaches us to teach one another, but that doesn't mean that we must speak over each other at the same time. "One another" does not demand "congregational," everyone ministering only reciprocally at the same time. It does not forbid *receiving* ministry when you are in need without *returning* equal ministry at the same instant.

- **Forgiving one another** (Eph 4:32 and Col 3:13). If you ask for my forgiveness, I will not wait until I need your forgiveness so that we can forgive one other at the same time. "One another" doesn't mean simultaneous.

- **Exhort one another daily** (Heb 3:13). The "one another" in this passage does not teach that all exhortation must be "congregational," everyone speaking at the same time. Moreover, if I can escape the debate, then the reciprocal sense may remind me of my accountability to encourage myself, even as I encourage others.

- **Speaking to one another in psalms** (Eph 5:19). Singing is not an attitude that never stops. I can let you minister to me and encourage me without having to sing to you at the same moment, whether in our homes or in an assembly.

- **Teaching and admonishing one another in psalms** (Col. 3:16). Let's see what Paul meant when he said to teach and admonish one another.

## Letting Paul Interpret Paul

In Colossians 3:16, Paul bids us to teach and admonish one another with all wisdom in our songs. Exclusion believes that Paul was saying that everyone must sing this teaching and admonition simultaneously. Interestingly enough, Paul uses the same Greek phrase ("teach and admonish with all wisdom") earlier in the same letter.

*We proclaim him, admonishing and teaching everyone with all wisdom, so that we may present everyone perfect in Christ.* (Colossians 1:18)

Here Paul speaks of his own practice of proclaiming Christ, "admonishing and teaching with all wisdom." When Paul taught and admonished, others listened; he did not demand that his listeners speak to him at the same instant. However, if Colossians 3:16 demands that Christians "teach and admonish in all wisdom" only by speaking at the same instant, then Paul's listeners would be required to speak to him as he spoke.

"One another" did not mean to act simultaneously to Paul.

Exclusion's mandate that we *all* sing whenever *anyone* sings is never stated in scripture, in either testament. It can hardly be deduced from the "one another" language of the Bible. There is nothing in the Bible to support the thought that "one another" must mean everyone speaking all at once only when Exclusion wants that meaning – only and always when words are *sung*. To the contrary, the Bible argues *for* individual singing in assemblies. Let's take a look.

## A New Testament Model for Assemblies

Now we are ready to hold our assemblies up to the New Testament model. If you wanted to know what singing in our assemblies should be like, where would you look? We have looked at New Testament passages on singing in our daily lives. We have considered the writings of early Christians that touched on singing God's praise, primarily during meals in their homes. Let's look now for New Testament passages that specifically claim to address our assemblies.

Paul discusses activity of the church when it "comes together" several times in 1 Corinthians. Here are some of his comments about those times in the church at Corinth.

- "...when you come together as a church, there are divisions among you" (11:18).

- "When you come together, it is not the Lord's Supper that you eat ..." (11:20).

- "...when you come together to eat, wait for each other. If anyone is hungry, he should eat at home..." (11:33, 34).

- "So if the whole church comes together and everyone speaks in tongues, and some who do not understand or some unbelievers come in, will they not say that you are out of your mind? But if an unbeliever or someone who does not understand comes in while everybody is prophesying, he will be convinced by all that he is a sinner.... (14:23, 24).

- "What shall we say, brothers? When you come together, everyone has a hymn, or a word of instruction, a revelation, a tongue or an interpretation. All of these must be done for the strengthening of the church. ... For you can all prophesy in turn so that everyone may be instructed and encouraged. ... If anyone thinks he is a prophet or spiritually gifted, let him acknowledge that what I am writing to you is the Lord's command." (14:26, 31, 37)

In these passages, Paul is talking about when the church comes together. He makes distinctions between these assembled times and what Christians might do at other times, including in their homes. He is talking about what *we* typically identify as "designated assemblies" or "public worship."

In 1 Corinthians 14:26, Paul talks about service that Christians may bring to an assembly. He fully anticipates that multiple Christians will bring a "hymn" [Greek: *psalmos*] or other word for the strengthening of the church. What does he mean? Take a moment to read all of 1 Corinthians 14.

Now, for a moment, let's put aside questions about the ability in our day to prophesy or speak in tongues. Let's think initially only about the church at Corinth. Regarding the ministries in 14:26, look to see if Paul said that the rules were different *only* for sharing a psalm. I think that you will find that they were not.

- Paul did not say that only the sharing of psalms had to be done with everyone speaking simultaneously, all at once.

- Paul did not forbid the actual *singing* of the psalm.

- Those who "had a hymn" were not told to save it instead for a home setting.

- Paul is not describing rare, extraordinary events, but rather what was expected.

- Paul did not ask that only the "most gifted" share a psalm in the assembly.

- Paul did not say that these were temporary rules to be set aside over time as the assembly grew in size.

It sounds like a solo, doesn't it? Jack Lewis concedes that in 1 Cor. 14:26 Paul was talking "about singing in the congregational assembly" and that "the passage makes clear that individual singing was done."[6] Since this passage does not mandate *exclusively* "congregational singing" at Corinth, it can hardly dictate *exclusively* "congregational singing" for us today. The passage instead commanded the church at Corinth to *allow* for individuals to share their psalms in the assembly. Period.

Paul doesn't merely tell us *that* an individual may sing a song in the assembly of God's people. Paul also tells us *why*. He tells us why room should be made for individuals to share a psalm in the assembly, and he is adamant: "If anyone thinks he is a prophet or spiritually gifted, let him acknowledge that what I am writing to you is the Lord's command."

In chapter 14, Paul discusses the gifts of prophecy and of tongues in the context of assemblies.

To speak in tongues, Paul says, is to speak (a) to God, for (b) self-edification (14:2, 4). But self-edification is *not* the purpose of the assembly. In contrast, everything must be done in God's assembly for the strengthening of the *church* (14:26). That's why tongues were *only* to be heard in an assembly if there was an interpreter (14:28; see also verses 16-19).

To prophesy, on the other hand, is to speak God's word (a) to *people*, for (b) *their* "strengthening, encouragement, and comfort" – to edify the church (14:3, 4). Those who shared God's word in the assembly, whether with a psalm, a word of instruction, or a revelation, were to "prophesy 'in turn' so that everyone may be instructed and encouraged" (14:31). Paul even noted that an unbeliever might come into the assembly and find "everybody" prophesying (14:24).

At Corinth, then, we are taken by the unmistakable anticipation in every assembly that God would move and lead. His Spirit continued to convict, enlighten, and reveal. Changed men would speak strength, encouragement, and comfort. The "order of worship" was not set, because God was present, and God was spontaneous, and God prepared whomever he chose. It was true then, wasn't it?

## Cookie Cutter Assemblies

The expectation that God would move in the assembly of his people faded after the early centuries. He was superseded by a program. Werner writes,

> *The first three centuries of the church witnessed many controversies; some of them concerned themselves directly with music. The most important of these issues were (a) organized versus spontaneous praying and singing; ...*
> **1. Organized versus spontaneous praying and singing.** *The best examples of this long-lasting controversy, whose results affected all church music, are offered by the various doxologies of the first three Christian centuries. ... The musical consequences of this process of standardization are obvious:* **organized prayer and chant gain a decided victory over spontaneous worship.** [emphasis mine, DRC][7]

The issue at Corinth was not about whether their exclusive song leader might plan three songs instead of only two before the opening prayer. It was rather a question of whether the church would exclude others from bringing their songs. Would Corinth let God move *in* their assemblies even as he moved *outside* of them?

It's a good question to ask about our assemblies today, isn't it? If the exclusion of solos was not the law for the church at Corinth, then when did it become the law at all? God is still present in our assemblies. God still desires to move in the assembly of his church, not just outside of our assemblies. In his respected book on worship, David Peterson encourages us with these words:

*Whatever conclusion we reach* [about spiritual gifts today], *1 Corinthians 14 surely speaks to us of the value and importance of spontaneous, verbal ministries of exhortation, comfort or admonition by congregational members (cf. 1 Thes. 4:18; 5:11, 14; Eph. 4:15). Such mutual ministry is often confined to the home group, or to times of personal interaction after church services. Why is it not also encouraged in the public gathering of the whole church? ... [T]here should be some space for the informal contributions of members.*[8]

## Exclusion's Clergy

1 Corinthians 14 addresses our assemblies, yet – as Peterson observes – we permit its commands **only outside** of our assemblies. To Exclusion, "a fitting and orderly way" (14:40) means "funneled through two or three special communicators." Rather than expecting God to speak through a variety of people **as we expect in other gatherings**, our assemblies establish our exclusive system of clergy.

- Our "best" speaker delivers almost every message. Even our elders prefer to address the full assembly through him. The "laity" may tell of God at home.

- Our "best" singer brings virtually every song – songs written by the world's most accomplished writers. The "laity" may share their song at home.

- A variety of men read scripture, but they read passages selected for them. They only read. If they want to share a different passage or make comment, they can do that at home.

- Prayer leaders are given their theme. They are often told what they are to "accomplish" with their prayer – how it fits into the day's topic. They are to pray, not preach.

- Some freedom is given the one who introduces the Lord's Supper, but even he must stay within the bounds of that meal. He can address other topics at home.

Instead of letting God speak to us through a variety of members, we avoid "surprises." We want the sparkle of the "best presentation" without the awkwardness of the unexpected.

In a 180-degree turn, *listening* as anyone shares a song in the assembly has become sin. The mandate that *all* singing be "congregational" further serves to bar the singing of any new song until it can be distributed and rehearsed. Miriam and Mary would have been told to wait. And no song may be introduced by any but the designated one or two singers.

No wonder so many decline to sing out, convinced that there is something unfit about the way that they sing. **We work on our pitch and our tempo and our syncopation and our dynamics, but that won't change our lives.** We may hear perfected harmonies, but we yearn to hear from convicted hearts. In truth, *we don't need to hear your song because you're the best singer, but because what God has taught you will make a difference to your brothers and sisters.* In the song that you (or we) are about to sing, we need to hear how God has been faithful to you. And we need to hear of his faithfulness from more than the same one or two week in and week out.

I mentioned earlier that I don't need all the fingers of one hand to count the Christians I personally know in the Churches of Christ who have written a song of praise. How many fingers do you need? Our fellowship does not encourage or cherish the song of our common brother. We have told others that their song has no place in our assembly – especially sung by them – for so long that they no longer believe that they *have* a song. And even if they had a song, they would never offer it in a setting where the standard is perfect renditions and critical review.

When we make no room in our assemblies for the song or testimony of the non-professional, we parallel the Apostles when they tried to keep the little children from coming to Jesus. Phillips, Craig, and Dean share a song called "His Favorite Song of All." In it, they remind us…

*It's not just melodies and harmonies that catches his attention.*
*It's not just clever lines and phrases that causes him to stop and listen,*
*But when any heart set free, washed and bought by Calvary begins to sing,*
*That's his favorite song of all.*[9]

In contrast to Corinth's day, our day describes assemblies with words like "worship leader" and "sermon." This language is not found in the New Testament. *God never limited our assemblies to the most talented.*

The limitation we place on who may sing parallels the limit we place on who may speak. Take a look at "preaching." Greek words for "preach" occur scores of times in the scriptures, but they are not found in 1 Cor. 14, the assembly passage. The most common New Testament words for "preaching" are *kērussō* (60 occurrences) and *ĕuaggĕlizō* (52 occurrences). They mean "to **herald** (as a public crier), especially divine truth,"[10] and "to announce good news (**'evangelize'**), especially the gospel,"[11] respectively. First century Christians preached "wherever they went" (Acts 8:4), and those who believed this preaching responded by being baptized (Acts 8:12). Paul wrote,

*How, then, can they call on the one they have not believed in? And how can they believe in the one of whom they have not heard? And how can they hear without someone preaching [heralding] to them? And how can they preach [herald] unless they are sent? As it is written, "How beautiful are the feet of those who bring good news [evangelize]!"* (Romans 10:14, 15)

Limiting the call to preach (herald and evangelize) to something done by one person primarily in our Sunday assemblies among the saved does not do justice to the first century pattern. Moreover, it has the unintended effect of convincing us that only one is qualified to share the gospel, in or out of the assembly. In my efforts to enlist Christians to read the Bible with Chinese college students, I learned that even gray-haired Christians hesitate to "evangelize" out of a fear that they will "mess things up." As a people, we are not persuaded that God can preach through us. Excluding others in favor of the "preferred" song leader and sermon-giver week after week hardly reflects first century practice. It is not what Paul laid down as "the Lord's command" for our assemblies.

We emphasize polish, but the Apostle Paul wasn't concerned about polish when *he* spoke. "When I came to you, brothers, I did not come with eloquence [KJV: 'excellency of speech'] or superior wisdom as I proclaimed to you the testimony about God... My message and my preaching were not with wise and persuasive words [KJV: 'enticing words of man's wisdom'], but with a demonstration of the Spirit's power, so that your faith might not rest on men's wisdom, but on God's power" (1 Cor. 2:1, 4, 5). When we come together, are we more anxious to see God move or to witness the eloquence of the "most capable" man? Ervin Bishop remarks,

> *There was no one person in any congregation considered so qualified as to be given the sole responsibility for the instruction and admonition of God's family. Even when Paul was present, he was joined by "many others" in both teaching and preaching (Acts 15:35). ...When only one or two members 'perform,' growth is stifled, and the body is crippled."*[12]

Can we truly say that we teach and admonish **"one another"** in our assemblies, or do the same two or three teach and admonish week after week, inviting us to sing along or occasionally to quote with them? Whatever group we are trying to reach, we hire "one of them" – a minority, a single, a young adult – to represent them before the assembly. The laity only speak when told to, and then only in unison. What a heavy burden we place on a select few!

## Exclusion's Old Testament Model

If our assemblies don't follow the model of Corinth, then what pattern *do* they follow? It is striking that our modern approach to singing more closely resembles singing in the first century temple than the singing in the first century church. The singing in the temple was rehearsed and refined. In Jesus' day, Levites trained for five years before they were authorized to sing in the choir.[13] The effect was impressive, though we should note that the untrained congregation was not invited to join in the song in the temple. As Lewis points out,

> *Worship in the temple was carried on by the priests and Levites, not by the congregation. Christians need to be careful that they do not project upon the temple their own concept of congregational worship. At its center, temple worship was not a congregational assembly; nevertheless, by custom people did gather in the courts at the time of sacrifice. The Levites did the singing.*[14]

We have adopted the model of the first century temple, except that we have invited the congregation to sing along. During the assembly, our rehearsed "clergy" does the teaching and admonishing. Opportunities for the congregation to teach and admonish are transferred to Bible classes and other small groups. We don't hear from those outside of our own small groups. We don't find the encouragement and inspiration of hearing about God's work in and through the lives of our common brothers and sisters in the assembly. We begin to judge the performance. We come to expect our favorite speaker and our favorite song leader and our favorite songs sung our way. It is the model that Exclusion teaches.

Whenever people say, "I didn't get much out of worship today" (meaning the assembly), we respond, "You get out of it what you put into it." For most of the church, what is "put into it" could as easily be put into an assembly that is watched on TV from home. Our Corinth comes before the assembly or after it (if at all), but not during. Exclusion touts "Congregational Singing" as necessary for the participation of all believers in our assemblies. From the perspective of Corinth, it is rather revealed as a way to prohibit participation. We need to make ourselves comfortable with the command that Paul laid down in all the churches.

Our assemblies replicate the rehearsed, professional practice of the temple, suppressing the unforeseen, un-scriptable, participative experience of the early church.

# Miracles Aside

When we began looking at 1 Corinthians 14, at first we only considered its meaning to the church at Corinth. We saw that Exclusion would not have been tolerated at Corinth. Why then would Exclusion outlaw solos today, given that they were protected at Corinth?

Some defenders of Exclusion argue that 1 Corinthians 14 does not apply to the church today because too much has changed since then, particularly with regard to the work of the Spirit. There is a broad spectrum of conclusions regarding how the Spirit may or may not be active in our day. For the sake of argument, let's say that 1 Corinthians 14 has absolutely no bearing on the singing in our assemblies today.

If that is true, then there is no other New Testament example of singing in an assembly. If passages on singing in our daily lives justify the abolition of solos in our assemblies, then they also abolish solos outside of our assemblies. But no one is ready to abolish solos in every setting, including song teaching or singing a song at home, as Mary did with Elizabeth. Exclusion might throw out 1 Corinthians 14, but it moves no closer to the establishment of only "congregational singing" only in assemblies.

Moreover, Paul's message was not unique to Corinth. It was "the Lord's command" (14:37). The Spirit was active in the churches of Ephesus and Colosse when Paul also told them to teach one another with their songs. He never commanded only simultaneous teaching, whether or not the words were sung. He did not instruct us to silence our brother until we could all sing along. His command to teach one another with our songs flies in the face of our command that only the same talented one or two bring every song.

Yes, we may pay a gifted teacher who has brought us God's word. 1 Corinthians 9:14 makes that clear. Yes, we may enlist a gifted musician to train our voices and guide us in song. But we also need to hear of

God's faithfulness from the lips of others. Hearing another bring his song in the assembly is something that God desires for us.

1 Corinthians 14 demanded that solos be allowed at Corinth. In contrast, there is nothing to demand *only* simultaneous, unison singing in the assembly. Neither is there any word to mandate an assembly clergy that speaks for the congregation. Instead, Paul anticipated Christians speaking "in turn" to build each other up. He anticipated the unexpected in the assembly.

**Were you surprised?** Did you already know that the word "congregational" doesn't occur in scripture? Were you surprised that our opposition to solos depended on a special interpretation of the phrase "one another" only for singing only during assemblies? Had you noticed before that the only New Testament passage that specifically addresses the songs of our assemblies approves solos but is "silent" on "congregational singing"?

**Who changed praise?** The Bible contradicts the teaching that we can only sing to "one another" if everyone speaks simultaneously. Scripture contradicts the teaching that only 1 or 2% of the congregation is qualified to bring a song to the assembly. When after first century Corinth did the church first practice the exclusion of solos? Who brought an end to individual singing in the assembly?

**Are you missing more than music?** Let God be our "worship leader" again. We can "speak to ourselves" with a song of God's praise even when we're all alone. And when we're all together, let's loosen our grip on the steering wheel of his assemblies. We can seek ways to let others compliment our principal speaker by sharing what God is teaching them as they faithfully apply his word. We can find ways to encourage others besides our principal song leader to introduce or sing the songs that mean something special to them this week. We can be impacted by the praise of numerous people rather than hearing ever through the lens of the same designated two or three. We can rejoice in the song of our tone-deaf brother just as his Father in Heaven does. We can welcome the "unexpected" again ... even in our assemblies. We must learn to be comfortable with God in control of our assemblies. Let's value what God says we need above what we have grown accustomed to.

Have you ever written down your praise? Have you made it into a poem or song of praise? If not, why not? If so, have you blessed others with it? Have you asked others to let you hear *their* song?

Let it be known that it is no sin to listen to praise.

---

[1] "The style of Jewish song is plain in the Magnificant…", Delling, p. 500.

[2] Though numerous people may have spoken out in early prayers, as Acts 4:24 perhaps indicates.

[3] Matt. 25:9, Luke 16:9; 21:30; Acts 13:46; Rom. 6:11; 12:19; I Cor. 3:18, etc.

[4] R. C. H. Lenski, p. 619.

[5] Moulton and Geden, *A Concordance to the Greek New Testament* (New York: Charles Scribner's Sons, 1897), pp. 240-244.

[6] "If Paul was talking only about individual singing rather than group singing, he was talking nevertheless about singing in the congregational assembly. The Gordian knot of the use of instrumental music in worship has not been affected. Since the passage makes clear that individual singing was done, it only focuses the question on whether instrumental music is authorized to accompany individual singing in the congregation." (Lewis, Ferguson, and West, *The Instrumental Music Issue*, p. 34).

[7] Werner, p.467.

[8] David Peterson, *Engaging with God*, Grand Rapids, MI: William B. Eerdmans Publishing Company, 1992, p 197.

[9] Phillips, Craig, & Dean. "Favorite Song of All." *Favorite Songs of All*. CD, Sparrow. 1998.

[10] James Strong, "A Concise Dictionary of the Words in the Greek New Testament," *The New Strong's Exhaustive Concordance of the Bible*. (Nashville: Thomas Nelson Publishers, 1984 (orig. 1890)), p 42.

[11] Strong, p. 33.

[12] Ervin Bishop, "The Christian Assembly (5)," *Firm Foundation*, 90, No. 32 (August 7, 1973), 7, 10.

[13] Olson, Lee G. *Music*, Ed. Merrill C. Tenney, *Zondervan Pictorial Bible Dictionary*. Grand Rapids, MI: Zondervan Publishing House, 1963, p. 566.

[14] Lewis, Ferguson, and West, p. 24.

# Exclusion's Fifth
## Disputable Matter:

## "God Desires Division
## When we Disagree over Praise"

# You Might Have a Man-Made Rule If...

How can you tell if something you believe is from God or from men?

It seems that nothing made Jesus angrier than when religious leaders replaced God's laws with their own. These leaders questioned Jesus' credentials as a rabbi because of the laws his disciples didn't keep. Yet when Jesus exploded at the Pharisees for their practice of replacing God's laws with their own, his own disciples still didn't get it. They actually asked Jesus if he realized that he was offending the Pharisees! (Matthew 15: 12) Jesus knew that these religious leaders could not be pleased and should not be appeased. He bluntly told his followers to forget the Pharisees (verse 13). Who can imagine a worse verdict?

No one wants to be guilty of enforcing man-made rules. We would NEVER do it on purpose. Our fear, however, is that we might not recognize a man-made rule for what it is. What gives us pause is the thought that we might enforce a man-made rule as though it were from God. This chapter attempts to help us identify the difference.

This chapter looks at four indications that a law might be from men. You might have a man-made rule if ...

1. ...men regulate when and how to apply it.

2. ...it is not clearly stated in scripture.

3. ...men promote it as the "safe" thing to do.

4. ...it claims silence where the Bible speaks.

## You might have a man-made rule if...
## 1. ...men regulate when and how to apply it.

Our college group was giving a report to one of our supporting congregations. After we were done in the auditorium, everyone was invited back to the fellowship hall for ice cream. It was also a chance for the church to see some of the skits our drama group performed out on the campus. I was really looking forward to it, because we had a talented group and some really great skits. On our way back to the fellowship hall, though, one of the deacons stopped me to say that there should not be any applause, because "applause for a Biblical message is not authorized in scripture." As I tried to get clarification, I learned that he didn't have a problem with us *performing* the skits. The problem was only with the clapping.

I was dumb-founded. I had thought that we were being very sensitive. We weren't performing in the auditorium. We were so far removed from a "designated assembly" that we were having ice cream. We wanted to make every concession, so I finally had to ask him if we should scrap our main skit for the evening – a game show that included a girl periodically holding up an "applause" sign. To my surprise, he said the skit could stay.

Of course, there is no clear rule in the Bible about when Christians can and cannot applaud. We can't look it up in the New Testament. The *only* way to know that you can applaud as a part of a skit but not because of a skit (or on the campus but not in the fellowship hall) is if men tell you. Men regulate applause; they let us know. They even break fellowship over it. It is a man-made rule.

In the first loophole chapter, we looked back to how our fellowship once used an Old Testament verse to oppose pants on women. Elderships began to rule on the exceptions. Most permitted little girls to wear shorts under their skirts at recess; though some narrowly ruled that girls should wear shorts under skirts *only* during recess. Others ruled that women could wear sweat suits to exercise if only women were present. God "detested" pants on women, but man regulated many exceptions. Men enforced their conclusions with church discipline. It was a man-made rule.

The pattern of regulation by men is no clearer anywhere than in our view of praise. As mentioned earlier, our system of exemptions and loopholes is the biggest problem that our young adults have with our approach to music. We would never do in a "designated assembly" many of the same things we do in our own VBS. We can listen to songs that praise God on a country station but not a Christian one. People can tap their foot to the beat in church, but they cannot clap. The two loophole chapters of this book give many, many examples. We have no consensus; there can be no consensus, because God does not say. Our regulation betrays the fact that our rules are man-made.

## You might have a man-made rule if...
## 2. ... it is not clearly stated in scripture.

My first "church" job was as a youth minister in a small East Texas town. I remember a man and his wife who were studying the Bible and decided that they wanted to be baptized. They had both been married once before. One of our deacons believed that their divorces lacked "scriptural grounds." He believed that if they were serious about repenting, then before they could be baptized they should dissolve their current marriage and attempt to reunite with their previous spouses. It was a common belief of the day. Of course, his conclusion flies in the face of Deuteronomy 24:1–4. It is also bizarre to say, "God hates divorce, so he wants you to get another one." Yes, God hates divorce, but the Bible never says that he doesn't *recognize* it.[1] Although the deacon was convinced of his position, he finally consented to the baptism, saying, "Let's baptize them just in case God will let them go to heaven." Thankfully, he could not enforce a rule that is not clearly stated in scripture.[2]

No Greek lexicon is more highly favored in our fellowship than *A Greek-English Lexicon of the New Testament and other Early Christian Literature*. Perhaps this is because **no one** makes a stronger pro-*a cappella* argument than its editor, Frederick Danker. As we have pointed out before, Danker introduces his comments regarding accompaniment in praise with these words: *"... although the New Testament does not voice opposition to instrumental accompaniment..."* Danker is stressing that his conclusions are not clearly stated in scripture.

Exclusion also must make this admission. God's people praised him with instruments throughout Jesus' life. John identifies worshippers praising God with accompaniment in three different chapters of his revelation. Similarly, as we have seen, the New Testament upholds solos rather than opposing them. Nowhere does God "voice opposition" to instruments or solos. Exclusion deduces rules that are not stated (or are arguably opposed) by the New Testament. It is a warning sign that we could be dividing over man-made rules.

The pioneers of the restoration movement insisted that we never require anything not clearly stated in scripture. Thomas Campbell argued that demanding others' obedience to my deductions from scripture is the unwarranted death knell of unity. In his *Declaration and Address*, he wrote,

> 6. *That although inferences and deductions from Scripture premises, when fairly inferred, may be truly called the doctrine of God's holy word, yet are they not formally binding upon the consciences of Christians farther than they perceive the connection, and evidently see that they are so; for their faith must not stand in the wisdom of men, but in the power and veracity of God. Therefore, no such deductions can be made terms of communion, but do properly belong to the after and progressive edification of the church. Hence, it is evident that no such deductions or inferential truths ought to have any place in the Church's confession.*[3]

I know a church that asks its elder candidates to fill out a questionnaire. One of my favorite questions is, "Have you changed your mind about any Biblical issue in the last 20 years? Explain." The thought is that someone who is a student of the word will answer, "Yes," and explain. How would you answer that same question? You won't say that you've changed your mind about who Jesus is or why he died; that is clear in scripture. However, you've probably changed your mind about some things you deduced that were not so clear. It is better never to break fellowship over such issues, because one day we might look back and say we were wrong.

If a thing is not clearly stated in scripture, then it is hard to distinguish a valid deduction from a law of men. Also, there is a difference between <u>preferring</u> *a cappella* praise (like Danker) and <u>demanding</u> *a cappella* praise *only* (like Exclusion). I may do what I deduce from scripture, but enforcing upon others what the Bible does not say is dangerous. It may be a sign of a man-made rule.

## You might have a man-made rule if...
## 3. ... men promote it as the "safe" thing to do.

Have you noticed how we divide when others will not adhere to what we see as the "safe" course? We are told that it is "safe" to use only one cup in the Lord's Supper, to not hire a youth minister, to not have Sunday school classes, to not have a kitchen in the church building (or to not have a church building at all), to not support orphans homes, to not celebrate Christmas, to not sing between the bread and the wine, to not support a "located" preacher, to not marry inter-racially, to not have small groups on Sunday nights, and on and on. Then we divide.

Exclusion defends splits by arguing that everyone should do what is *safe*. "We know that we can sing all together and without instruments," Exclusion reasons, "so shouldn't we do that and nothing more? Surely we can all agree to do what is *safe* for the sake of unity. Those who allow instruments and solos elevate their desires above unity."

Is there a scriptural precedent for "playing it safe?" Is safety the path to unity? Jesus addresses this issue in Mark 7:1-23. The Pharisees asked Jesus why his disciples didn't ceremonially wash their hands before eating. Would you have washed your hands ... for the sake of unity? After all, washing your hands is "safe," isn't it? There is no harm in washing your hands. If everyone had ceremonially washed their hands, then that issue would not have caused division.

You know how Jesus answered. He said that it is *never* safe to bind what God has not required upon others. The issue is not if it is a sin to wash your hands or to sing *a cappella*. The issue is if I can demand that you **must** ceremonially wash or sing only congregationally and *a cappella.* Can Exclusion (in its various forms) demand that others *only* do what it has deduced … for the sake of unity? In other words, are you required to obey what I think is safe, in absence of a clear command from God, in order for us to have unity?

Jesus said that the answer is always "no." It might have appeared "safe" to wait until Sunday to heal the withered hand, but Jesus refused (Mark 3:1-6). It might have appeared "safe" to circumcise Titus, but Paul refused: *"Yet not even Titus, who was with me, was compelled to be circumcised, even though he was a Greek. This matter arose because some false brothers had infiltrated our ranks to spy on the freedom that we have in Christ and to make us slaves"* (Gal. 2:3-4). Paul did not tolerate shackles.

When others cannot see your point of view, and you resort to contending that your conclusions are the only "safe" ones, watch out. That line of reasoning goes with rules of men. **Those who withhold unity for the sake of "safety" wish to make others their slaves.** True unity only comes with freedom. Absent a clear command from God, each of us must do what we believe is right without condemning those who disagree. Freedom is the scriptural precedent (Romans 14).

## You might have a man-made rule if...
## 4. ... it claims silence where the Bible speaks.

Exclusion argues that instruments and solos are not mentioned in the New Testament, so they are not authorized. It says that they are prohibited by silence. To the contrary, as we have seen, the New Testament is *not* silent on solos and accompaniment in our praise.

The only New Testament passage to specifically address singing in our assemblies is 1 Corinthians. 14. In that passage, Paul anticipates the singing of solos. We can sing in unison in our assemblies because of the freedom of silence, but the New Testament is not silent on solos in the assembly.

Neither is the New Testament silent on instrumental accompaniment in our praise. The New Testament gives us examples of accompanied praise, prophecy of accompanied praise, and vocabulary of accompanied praise. This isn't silence!

Exclusion trumps everything that *is* written by asserting what is *nowhere* written – that singing must be "congregational" and *a cappella* only in our assemblies.

## Traditions

Of course, not every tradition is wrong. We can practice something without binding it. It is one thing to say that we meet at 10 AM because it is our tradition; it is another thing to say we meet at 10 AM because the Bible demands that hour, that we question the faith of those who meet at other hours, or that those who prefer another hour are unfit for leadership in our 10 AM churches.

In the same way, church leaderships can honor our singing tradition without implying that it is Biblically mandated. After discussing the topic in private, our leaders cannot afford to veil their conclusions. They can no longer pronounce carefully worded judgments that hope by their vagueness to offend no one. The flock seeks a model of clarity, openness and freedom. Our flocks deserve the honesty of discussing *why* we sing *a cappella*. We can sing *a cappella* (or meet at 10 AM) without insisting that it is commanded by God.

The Apostle Paul warns us not to pass judgment on "disputable matters" (Romans 14:1). Our opposition to accompaniment and solos has all the markings of a disputable matter. It is not clearly stated in scripture. Men regulate how and when to apply it because the Bible does not say. The best many can do is merely to enforce what Exclusion determines is safe. Arguably, Exclusion defers to history despite what is written in scripture.

Did you notice how we ignore these warning signs on almost everything that divides the church? We will look deeper into the impact on unity in the next chapter.

***Were you surprised?*** Did you notice how we use the same flawed pattern to divide Christ's church over issue after issue? I'm sure you could add your own examples to the ones in this chapter. Think about the times in your life when you've been surprised by disputes in the church. Notice how many of the warning signs of man-made rules were present.

***Discover unity!*** The pioneers of the restoration movement would not bind *a cappella* singing *only* in our praise. They preached freedom. As the New Testament taught them, they would not bind their deductions. We also must renounce the practice of drawing lines in the sand over disputable matters. Paul refused the shackles. Jesus refused the shackles. The leaders of the restoration / unity movement refused the shackles. We also must refuse the shackles.

Just as important, this chapter reminds us that we must refuse to take part in binding others in *our* shackles. We cannot even be a silent partner in that practice. We must abandon the false Gods of deduction and safety. We must lead the call for freedom in Christ.

***Are you missing more than music?*** Thank God for unity that allows diversity! Praise him for a Holy Spirit within us to teach us and to convict us. Let the Holy Spirit do what the Holy Spirit alone *can* do. Thank God for grace to forgive us when we see that we have been wrong. Unity is knocking on our door.

---

[1] Indeed, Jesus told the woman at the well that she had had *five* husbands (John 4:18). Are you thinking now that all 5 *must* have died on her?

[2] An EXCELLENT book on the divorce issue is *Marriage & Divorce (revised edition),* by John L. Edwards (Joplin, MO: College Press, 1985).

[3] Thomas Campbell, *Declaration and Address.* (St. Louis, Missouri: Mission Messenger, 1972), p. 46.

# Is It Worth Splitting the Church?

Many today conclude that the Bible and the early church are at ease with and even welcome instruments and solos. Exclusion's final objection, then, is that their use may split the church. Exclusion's perspective is that instruments split the church before, and acceptance of them today threatens to split the church again. There is, however, a competing perspective.

On one occasion, Jesus was invited to eat at the house of a Pharisee. The problems began before Jesus took his first bite. "But the Pharisee, noticing that Jesus did not first wash before the meal, was surprised" (Luke 11:28). Jesus' response is known in Luke as "six woes" pronounced upon the Pharisees and experts in the law. One might ask whether Jesus caused division by *not washing* as the Pharisees required OR if the Pharisees caused division by requiring Jesus to wash.

Regarding division over instruments and solos, there are also two perspectives. This chapter asks if it is their use or their prohibition that has already split the church, and what the consequences of that split are. We will look at unity and then at the cost of our division.

## Unity

Concern over splitting the church is a very worthy consideration. The unity of God's people is demanded over and over in the pages of scripture. Jesus said that our unity would testify that God had sent him (John 17:21). Paul said that it doesn't matter how we sing or do anything else if we don't have love (1 Cor. 13:1-3), and he routinely condemned division. He said that we had no business judging another man's servant (Romans 14:4). James warned us not to slander one another (4:11) judge one another (4:12), or grumble against one another lest we be judged, for "The judge is standing at the door" (5:9). The unity and love of believers is paramount in scripture.

Our religious movement, therefore, was once known as a *unity* movement. Godly men intent on the union of God's people led a call for unity that swept the United States. They counseled Christians to let go of their man-made creeds and to enter into communion together.

A lot has changed since we split over the instrument. There has been no end to our splitting and splintering. No one calls us a "unity" movement any more. There's hardly any resemblance of that today. "Is it worth splitting the church?" Regardless of what "it" is, **our movement has forgotten how to say "no."** Of our divisions, Carl Ketcherside wrote a generation ago,

> *One faction accuses those who defend the use of individual cups as preaching another gospel; a second accuses those who employ Bible classes as preaching another gospel; a third labels those who support "Herald of Truth" as preaching another gospel; while those who support this international propaganda medium denounce those who believe in the premillennial coming of Jesus as preaching another gospel. The non-instrument segment of the restoration movement has disintegrated into a group of clamoring camps and clashing clans, slashing at each other over radio and from behind paper curtains, all blasting away at the others as having "perverted the gospel."* [1]

Today, we – the Churches of Christ – *are* a splintering splinter. Division over instruments caused one split, and we've gone on to splinter time and again. The Bible speaks volumes against division. It has little to say (if anything) in support of our divisions over solos and instruments, multiple cups, church ownership of buildings, Bible classes, small groups on Sunday nights, and singing during the Lord's supper, etc. Once the spirit of Exclusion gets a taste of having its way, there appears to be no way to satisfy it. **Our anti-instrument, anti-solo stance is the tip of Exclusion's iceberg.**

The question is not, "Is it worth *splitting* the church?" but rather, "Is it worth *remaining* shattered?" Is our allegiance to Exclusion – in each of its varied forms – worth all the splits in the church?

## The Cost of our Division: What is at Stake

1) At stake is the evangelism of a lost world. One of Christ's sentinel concerns was that His followers be one. Why? Because all men would know that God had sent Him if we were united. (John 17:20, 21) Unity is a sign, because only God can make self-seeking humans behave as one. Instead, we have resisted. We have sacrificed what Jesus explicitly asks of us (unity) in deference to what some say he meant us to infer regarding singing. We have taken our eyes off of the bull's eye in order to aim at something that is apparently not even on His target.

We value the unity of our movement above the unity of the church of God. In the face of our call to a lost world, some are more concerned about keeping our severed finger intact than about reattaching it to the body. We concern ourselves with the unity of our splinter and sacrifice the unity of Christ's body. Jesus said that unity is the ultimate proof to the non-believer that he was sent by God. It is that important.

2) At stake is our influence and inclusion in the full, intended fellowship of Christ's church on earth. Because we cannot participate with other believers in what is, after prayer, the simplest act of communal worship, we relegate ourselves to a self-imposed quarantine. As others discuss weighty matters, we are absent from the table. We are AWOL as our brothers and sisters discuss being born again, the work of the Spirit, providence, perseverance, congregational autonomy and interdependence, evangelism, and on and on. (Even if we have an occasional ear in the church at large, our brothers will always be skeptical of our reasoning abilities on other subjects as long as we cling to our infamous, indefensible view on music.) We have no relationships out of which to hear or be heard because in a great part our view of

music has removed us from the relationships forged while worshiping together.

A Baptist minister and friend once asked of me, "Danny, tell me what you believe about baptism, because I have never before had a friend in the Churches of Christ that I could ask." That is what we are missing.

If the church at large is the lesser for our absence, so also are we. We are not called from our apathy by the zeal of other believers. We are not sharpened by one another's questions and challenges. We neither give nor receive the blessings that Christ would otherwise bestow in His full body. As a nation is rocked by God's movement through groups like Promise Keepers and Bible Study Fellowship, we sit home because of an issue of our own invention.

3) At stake are our future converts, including our own biological children. Our converts include internationals who return home to no church at all if they must find an anti-instrument Church of Christ with the correct suite of other "anti" issues. Our converts include those in our mission points where Christians are few and the need for fellowship is high.

Our converts include our own children who walk away looking for an assembly where they say they feel the presence of God. They wonder why our churches ask them to tell their stories and sing their songs and raise (or clap) their hands out of sight. They deeply yearn to hear what God has done in your life, and think you might be blessed to hear of his hand in theirs. They aren't sure where we got the blueprint for our assemblies. They can attend concerts to find better singing, but they keep looking to interact with other hearts. In the worst cases they walk away and quit looking.

\* \* \* \* \*

Too much is at stake. No, it is not time to split the church, but time to fight for its healing. It is time to call for freedom in Christ. It is time to calmly look at the evidence and openly, persistently, unashamedly expect the *freedom from opinions that gives life to unity*. No, instruments and solos won't save us. We must not exclude *a cappella* or "congregational" singing, but we MUST quit sacrificing unity because of our desire to exclude instruments and solos. It is time for a splintered church to heal.

***Who changed praise?*** There is never a word from Jesus, his apostles, other inspired writers, or church fathers across the first four centuries to say that God changed his mind about solos or accompaniment (instruments and clapping) in our songs of his praise at any time, let alone only during assemblies. To the contrary, the Bible is not silent on solos and accompaniment in our praise, and what it has to say defends them.

"Who changed praise?" we asked. IT WASN'T GOD. That's what matters.

***Discover Unity!*** Many of the issues that divide us are heralded as sound doctrine, though they are not clearly stated in scripture. In contrast, it *is* clear that ***unity is sound doctrine***. Let us vacate the judgment seat. The command for unity is accomplished when we defend freedom in Christ. May the numbers of our churches bear witness that we encourage diversity, not that we banish it. Let us be known as the unity movement once more!

Every Sunday in the assembly where I attend, we have a unity prayer. We rotate through the phone book, specifically praying for three different churches each week. Praying for unity is a good first step.

***Are you missing more than music?*** Thank God as we break the shackles that we have placed on others and that others have placed on us. In this way, let us discover praise and unity as we have never known them before!

---

[1] Ketcherside, W. Carl, *Mission Messenger*, January 1965, as quoted by Tom Burgess, *Documents on Instrumental Music* (College Press, 1966), p. 115.

# Setting Aside Our Gift at the Altar

God would rather that his church be unified than to hear the most beautiful song we could offer him. If we are about to offer him our song, and remember that we have wronged a fellow believer, then God asks us to hold our song until we have made things right with our brother.[1] He says that our relationships are that important.

When you began reading this book, perhaps you knew that the questions about instruments or solos were not the tough questions. Our study has naturally focused attention on what is truly difficult. The hardest part (as always) is how we *respond* to our study. Where the rubber meets the road is in the doing, not the knowing.

It is unthinkable to pretend that division is not a problem. Neither can we let ourselves be tempted to say that the jury is still out. May God forgive us if we are hopeful that someone, somewhere, somehow will come up with a valid argument for breaking fellowship over *a cappella*, congregational singing. May God forgive us if we would rather save face than repent. It is a serious thing to divide the church of God. He expects us to make things right with the brothers we have shut out over worship. He expects us to acknowledge the pain we have caused.

Whenever God asks us to do something difficult, we are tempted to make excuses. We rationalize a limited response. We suggest that ours is a special case. We say, "God said so, but what if ...?"

- What if this confession is costly?
- What if my repentance destroys relationships?
- What if my obedience escalates the fracturing of churches?
- What if orphanages are caught in the middle?
- What if missions suffer critical cutbacks in support?

We become worst-case-scenario Christians, questioning whether God is able to handle the fallout from what he has asked us to do. We offer to help him out by doing less than he asks.

Since God asks us to focus on the good,[2] maybe we should consider some other "what ifs?"

- What if my confession heals relationships rather than destroys them?
- What if my sacrifice stops the flow of Christians leaving our churches?
- What if my repentance unites churches, bringing fracturing to an end?
- What if I am caught by surprise and am blessed by what God asks of me?
- What if faithful churches rise to the aid of ministries that suffer?
- What if God provides for ministers who trust him more than they fear the future?
- What if the unity movement becomes the unity movement again?
- What if God is in control?

We have cause to be best-case-scenario Christians.

We *will* say, "I was wrong," one day. The only question is if it will be in this life. I would rather do it by faith now because I want to see God work *now*. I am ready to say, "I'm sorry."

I am ready to hear the song of Zechariah.[3] I am going to watch his face as he bursts with the news of what God has done for him. God gave him his song and his voice;[4] it is not man's place to silence either. So, I won't substitute someone else "more gifted" to sing his song instead. I'll continue to sing with the song leader, and I'll buy his CDs, but I'm going to hear Zechariah's song on Zechariah's lips, first hand. Neither will I put him off until his song can be "properly" rehearsed or published. We will sing it with him soon enough. I look forward to that, too.

I intend to witness the drama of Agabus. When he pulled off Paul's belt and bound himself, the church was brought to tears.[5] I want God's message made real to me just like that. I want it burned into my mind's eye. Examples from prophets like Ezekiel and Hosea and Jesus[6] and Agabus confirm that God loves teaching visually with drama, with living parables. Teach me with flannel graphs and puppets and drawings on white boards. Move me with skits and videos, even as you teach me with without them. I'm going to learn with my eyes as well as my ears.

I hope to dance with the once-crippled man. The apostles made no effort to contain or rebuke him as he jumped about, praising God.[7] If they would not stop him then, why would we stop him today? I was crippled once, too, weren't you? I won't ask you to dance, but I yearn to witness his dance. I am very inhibited, but if I jump for joy, I don't want to fear that you will turn away from me.

I want to pursue worship in my daily life and passion in my praise. I want to hear testimonies of God's work in the assembly of his people, whether it is sung or not.

I want to learn how to disagree, because I want to embrace Christians who disagree on disputable matters.[8] Indeed, I pledge to defend them.[9] I commit to never drive my sons away over debatable conclusions. I want to know the blessings of being one with you in Christ. I want to end this long night of division.

In its place, I want to welcome the dawn of the day of multiplication. I am ready for a lost world to come to Jesus because of a church that is united.[10] I want to see them drawn in amazement at what God alone can do. I want to be in that number.

I am ready to offer my gift at the altar. When I say, "I was wrong," someone may gloat, but someone else is going to answer, "I've missed you. I thank God to count you as a brother." I want to restore those relationships in Christ.

So here goes. I'm sorry. Forgive me and accept my hand. We've been missing more than music.

[1] Matthew 5:23-24.
[2] Philippians 4:8.
[3] Luke 1:67-79.
[4] Luke 1:64.
[5] Acts 21:10-14.
[6] Ezekiel 12, all of Hosea, and John 13:1-17, respectfully, to name a few examples.
[7] Acts 3:6-10.
[8] Romans 14:1
[9] Mark 9:38-41
[10] John 17:21

# Appendix:

# My Song

I mentioned in chapter one that I love to write songs. As I said then, I don't believe I have ever led a Vacation Bible School or a Leadership Training for Christ chorus without teaching songs that I have written or arranged. You may remember that one year, one of the kids asked me to teach her how I write songs, and I did. That year, our chorus sang the song that she had written, and we loved it. Her dad thanked me and wondered why we don't encourage our kids to write songs of praise. I realized that I didn't need all the fingers of one hand to count those I knew in the Churches of Christ who had written a song of praise.

The song I am sharing is called, "Wasting Time." The text for it comes from Psalm 127, a short psalm of only five verses. I was initially drawn to the psalm because of what it said about children, how they were a blessing from the Lord. My wife and I had a lot of trouble having children, and I once wondered why God might be withholding the blessing spoken of in verses 3-5. While I prayed over those verses, I was also drawn to the first two verses of the psalm. They intrigued me as they reminded me that God is the one who cares for us and gives us rest. Those are the words I set to music.

By the way, my wife and I are blessed to have two sons today.

Anyway, maybe hearing one of my songs will encourage you to write down a song of your own ... and share it. I pray my song blesses you.

# Wasting Time
## Psalm 127

words and music by
Danny Corbitt

time.
time

For God provides for those he loves
For you provide for those you love

1. E -ven
2. E -ven

e -ven while they sleep.
e -ven while we sleep

For God provides for
For you provide for

those he loves,
those you love,

and he gives them sleep.-----
and you give us sleep.-----

D.C. al CODA    ⊕ CODA

sleep. -----    time.

I'm done with wasting my

time
wasting my time.

I'm done with wasting my time.

167

# Bibliography

Allen, Leonard and Lynn Anderson, editors. *The Transforming of a Tradition*. Orange, CA: New Leaf Books, 2001.

Atchley, Rick and Bob Russell, *Together Again,* Abilene, TX: Leafwood Publishers and Cincinnati, OH: Standard Publishing, 2006.

Arndt, William F. and Gingrich, F. Wilbur, editors, *A Greek-English Lexicon of the New Testament and other Early Christian Literature*, (based on Walter Bauer's fourth edition, 1952), Chicago: University of Chicago Press, 1957.

Barnes, Albert, *Notes on the Old Testament; Psalms, 3 Vols.* Grand Rapids, MI: Baker Book House, 1950.

Bishop, Ervin, "The Christian Assembly (2)," *Firm Foundation*, 90, No. 10 (March 13, 1973). 1973

Bishop, Ervin, "The Christian Assembly (5)" *Firm Foundation*, 90, No. 32 (August 7, 1973), 7, 10. 1973.

Botterweck, G. Johannes and Ringgren, Helmer, editors, *A Theological Dictionary of the Old Testament*, 12 vols. Trans. David Green. Grand Rapids, Michigan: William B. Eerdmans Publishing Company, 1980.

Burgess, Tom, *Documents on Instrumental Music,* College Press, 1966.

Campbell, Thomas, *Declaration and Address.* St. Louis, Missouri: Mission Messenger, 1972.

Cook, J. M, *The Bible Commentary; I Samuel – Esther,* Grand Rapids, Michigan: Baker Book House, 1953.

Carlisle, Bob. "Butterfly Kisses." *Butterfly Kisses (Shades of Grace).* CD. Benson (0124 1 41613 2 1). 1997.

Danker, Frederick William, editor, *A Greek-English Lexicon of the New Testament and other Early Christian Literature*, third edition (based on Walter Bauer's sixth edition), Chicago: University of Chicago Press, 2000

Davidson, Benjamin, *The Analytical Hebrew and Chaldee Lexicon*, Grand Rapids, Michigan: Zondervan Publishing House, 1970 (orig. work 1848).

Edwards, John L., *Marriage & Divorce (Revised Edition)* Joplin, MO: College Press, 1985.

Ferguson, Everett, *A Cappella Music in the Public Worship of the Church (Revised Edition)* Abilene, Texas: Biblical Research Press, 1972.

*Gesenius' Hebrew and Chaldee Lexicon to the Old Testament Scriptures*, trans. Samuel Prideaux Tregelles, Grand Rapids, MI: Baker Book House, 1979.

Gilbrant, Thoralf, editor, *Old Testament Hebrew-English Dictionary.* 17 vols., Springfield, MO: World Library Press Inc., 1996.

Gingrich, F. Wilbur and Danker, Frederick W., editors, *A Greek-English Lexicon of the New Testament and other Early Christian Literature*, second edition (based on Walter Bauer's fifth edition, 1958), Chicago: University of Chicago Press, 1979

*Harding University Graduate School of Religion Bulletin*, 39, No. 1 (January 1998)

*Interpreter's Dictionary of the Bible.* Nashville, TN: Abingdon Press, 1984.

Jennings, William, *Lexicon to the Syriac New Testament (Peshitta)*, London: Oxford at the Clarendon Press, 1926.

Jones, Milton, *The Other Side of the Keyboard*, Joplin, MO: College Press, 2005.

Josephus, *The Works of Josephus: New Updated Edition.* Trans. William Whiston. Peabody, Massachusetts: Hendrickson Publishers, 1987.

Koehler, Ludwig and Baumgartner, Walter, *The Hebrew and Aramaic Lexicon of the Old Testament*, New York: E. J. Brill, 1994.

Lenski, R. C. H., *The Interpretation of Saint Paul's Epistles to the Galatians, Ephesians, and Philippians.* Minneapolis, MN: Augsburg Publishing House, 1961.

Lewis, Jack P., "A Cappella Worship in the Assembly," *Harding University Graduate School of Religion Bulletin*, 39, No. 1 (January 1998), p. 1.

Lewis, Jack P., Ferguson, Everett, and West, Earl, *The Instrumental Music Issue*, Nashville, TN: The Gospel Advocate Co., 1987.

Liddell, Henry George and Scott, Robert, compilers, *A Greek-English Lexicon.* Oxford: Clarendon Press, 1968

Louw, Johannes P. and Nida, Eugene A., editors, *Greek-English Lexicon of the New Testament based on Semantic Domains,* second edition, New York: United Bible Societies, 1988.

McKinnon, James, *Music in Early Christian Literature.* Cambridge: Cambridge University Press, 1987.

McKinnon, James, *The Temple, the Church Fathers and Early Western Chant,* Aldershot, Hampshire, Great Britain: Ashgate Publishing Limited, 1998.

Moulton, F.W. and Geden, A. S., *A Concordance to the Greek New Testament,* New York: Charles Scribner's Sons, 1897.

Moulton, James Hope, and Milligan, George, *The Vocabulary of the Greek Testament.* London: Hodder and Stroughton, Linited, 1930.

*New Encyclopædia Britannica,* Chicago: Encyclopædia Britannica, Inc., 32 vols., 2005.

*New Testament Greek-English Dictionary,* Springfield, MO: The Complete Biblical Library. New Testament, vols. 11-16, 1991.

Peterson, David, *Engaging with God.* Grand Rapids, MI: William B. Eerdmans Publishing Company. 1992.

Phillips, Craig, & Dean. "Favorite Song of All." *Favorite Songs of All.* CD, Sparrow (7243 8 20210 2 5), 1998.

Rabin, Haim, *A Comprehensive Etymological Dictionary of the Hebrew Language for Readers of English.* New York: MacMillan Publishing Company, 1987.

Robinson, Edward, *A Hebrew and English Lexicon of the Old Testament* based on the lexicon of William Gesenius. Oxford: Clarendon Press, 1953 (original 1907).

Sheerer, Jim and Williams, Charles L., editors, *Directions for the Road Ahead: Stability in Change Among the Churches of Christ.* Chickasha, Okla.: Yeoman Press, 1998.

Smith, J. Payne, editor, *A Compendious Syriac Dictionary,* London: Oxford at the Clarendon Press, 1903.

Strong, James, *The New Strong's Exhaustive Concordance of the Bible.* Nashville: Thomas Nelson Publishers, 1984.

Tennery, Merrrill C., Gen. Ed., *The Zondervan Pictorial Bible Dictionary.* Grand Rapids, MI: Zondervan Publishing House, 1963.

Thayer, Joseph Henry, *A Greek-English Lexicon of the New Testament*, from *Grimm's Wilke's Clovis Novi Testamenti*. Grand Rapids, MI: Baker Book House, 1977.

*Theological Dictionary of the New Testament*, Ann Arbor, Michigan: Wm. B. Eerdman's Publishing Co., 10 vols, 1972.

Way International, The, *The Concordance to the Peshitta Version of the Aramaic New Testament*, New Knoxville, Ohio: American Christian Press, 1985.

*Webster's Ninth New Collegiate Dictionary*, Springfield, Massachusetts: Merriam-Webster Inc., 1987.

Wingram, George V., *The Analytical Greek Lexicon of the New Testament*. Peabody Massachusetts: Hendrickson Publishers, 1968.

Zodhiates, Spiros, *The Complete Word Study Dictionary, New Testament*. Chattanooga, TN: AMG Publishers, 1992.

# About the Author

Danny Corbitt grew up in Duncanville, a suburb of Dallas. In his youth, he spent several years at the local Christian Church and then began attending the Church of Christ nearby. He experienced the worship differences that not only set the groups apart, but also kept them apart.

Danny has worked as a youth minister, a missionary, and a state college minister for the Churches of Christ. He was a summertime youth minister in East Texas during his undergraduate years at the University of Texas at Arlington. Graduate school at Abilene Christian University prepared him for his mission work in Santiago, Chile. Shortly after his return, he began serving as a campus minister at his alma mater, UT Arlington. He served there for 14 years. In 2000, he left supported ministry and returned to work as a computer programmer, coding primarily in Visual Basic, C# and SQL.

Danny and his wife, the former Cindy Russell, have been married for over 20 years. They and their sons Cason and Austin love music. Cason is an alternate to the Texas All-State Choir this year, and Austin regularly plays drums in the church praise band.

The Corbitt's church family is Christ Community Church in Arlington, Texas. Over the years, CCC has joined hands with traditional Churches of Christ, sharing in youth events and Leadership Training for Christ, etc. While at CCC, Danny has written the computer software that manages the benevolent outreach of Arlington's Churches of Christ. Besides this involvement with Churches of Christ, CCC also participates with other churches. They sing accompanied and a cappella, and every Sunday they pray for unity.

CPSIA information can be obtained at www.ICGtesting.com
Printed in the USA
LVOW11s1624030215

425517LV00001B/313/P

9 781434 343598